POLISH
FIRST
NAMES

POLISH
FIRST
NAMES

Sophie Hodorowicz Knab

HIPPOCRENE BOOKS, INC.
New York

ISBN 0-7818-0749-2

For information, address:
HIPPOCRENE BOOKS, INC.
171 Madison Avenue
New York, NY 10016

Printed in the United States of America.

CONTENTS

INTRODUCTION

CHOOSING the name of a child is as important today as it was centuries ago, and should be given much thought and consideration. After all, it is a child's name that will set him or her apart from others. Often, it is the first word a child will learn to speak.

Every nation possesses its own unique treasury of names to draw upon when a newborn arrives. Yet, there is more historical and cultural significance to naming a child than one might think. Specifically, this book is aimed to help one become acquainted with both modern and traditional Polish first names. It also importantly highlights the etymological and historical influences that have led to the use and popularity of these names.

Polish names are derived from two major time periods: from ancient times until the acceptance of Christianity in 966 A.D., and from 966 A.D. to the present. The former includes native names categorized as Old Polish or Slavic in origin. During this early period, people lived in nomadic clans and tribes, hunting and gathering, and faced numerous environmental dangers as well as tribal enemies. It was strongly believed that a child would develop the characteristics of whomever or whatever he/she was named after. Thus, the selection of a name was a truly serious affair. The child would need a strong name—a name

1

with honor, and rich with history and promise. Commonly, these "strong" names were formed by combining significant root words. For example, the name *Władysław* comes from the Polish roots *włād* "ruler" and *sław* "fame, glory, renown." Joined together, the name depicts a famous or glorious ruler. These combined names have few English equivalents, although many Polish names such as *Władysław* and *Stanisław* were erroneously changed to Walter and Stanley at Ellis Island or in American schools.

The second group of names dates from Poland's acceptance of Christianity in 966 A.D. until the present. During this time, the Church required individuals to receive baptismal names with Christian significance. At baptism, when they were "born again," early Christians assumed new personal names—invariably the names of exemplary people and saints who had gone before them. Popular Polish names such as *Krzysztof* and *Magdalena* can be traced back to the Old and New Testaments.

The Church appointed certain calendar days as belonging to certain saints. There are literally thousands of saints, many with the same first name; and, many feast days vary from diocese to diocese or from one religious order to another. In Europe, throughout the Middle Ages, it was customary to name an infant after the saint upon whose feast day he or she had been born. (In this book, the feast dates given for each name are those most commonly accepted; they are indicative of the date of the saint's death or the translation date of his/her relics.) If the saint's name was suitable and pleased the parents and family, it was used. However, if the parents wanted another name, the name of a saint whose feast day had already passed was chosen.

2

This ensured that the infant would fall immediately under that saint's protection. Parents who did not adhere to the rules chose a name the family desired without any regard to the calendar. But, the name was always a Catholic one, derived from the Old or New Testament or from the lives of the saints.

The custom of naming a child after a saint led to the celebration of that saint's day as the child's "name day" or "feast day." In many parts of Europe, including Spain, Italy, France and Poland, celebrating the name day was far more important than celebrating the actual date of birth. The name day, called *imieniny* in Polish, signified the feast of the saint whose name was received in baptism.

This "baptismal" saint became, in essence, the child's hero or heroine and a special patron throughout life. As a child matured, he or she was told of the stories and legends relating to his/her special saint. The child was instructed to pray to the saint every day for help and guidance, and to derive inspiration from that saint's kind acts towards others.

In this book, diminutive names are also included. Christian name diminutives often become the "pet names" or "nicknames" used within the family and by close friends as terms of endearment. Some of the ancient Polish spellings would make for unique names themselves.

An increasing number of third and fourth generation Polish Americans are changing their first and last names back to original family names. And as they, too, become parents, they are choosing first and middle names for their children which reflect their Polish heritage. Why not ask grandparents, great-grandparents and relatives about the background and significance of

3

their names? One of the key needs of young people today is a source of identity, of knowing who they are and where they came from. They need heroes and heroines in their lives, whether it is a grandmother who traveled alone in steerage to begin a new life in America, or a 14TH century saint whose life was devoted to the care of the sick and the poor.

GIRLS' NAMES

Ada. Ada. German. Derived from **Adelajda** (Adelaide),
   Adela or Adelina. "Nobility."
   DIMINUTIVE: None
   FEAST DAY: July 7

❖ ❖ ❖

Adela. Adela. Old German. Derived from **Adelajda**
   (Adelaide). "Nobility."
   Appeared in Polish documents from 1267. Not a common
   name today.
   DIMINUTIVE: Adelka
   FEAST DAYS: January 3, November 23, December 24

❖ ❖ ❖

Adelajda. Adelaide. Old German. "Nobility."
   A name given to many Polish princesses in the Piast
   Dynasty. It was also the name of many queens of Poland,
   including the wives of Bolesław III (1086–1138) and
   Kazimierz III the Great (1310–1370).
   DIMINUTIVES: Adela, Adelka
   FEAST DAYS: February 5, June 11, December 16

❖ ❖ ❖

Agata. Agatha. Greek. "Good."

Appeared in Polish writings in the 13ᵀᴴ century as *Agata*
and *Jagata*. A favorite name in the small country villages
of Poland until the 18ᵀᴴ century, and then came into favor
again in the 1970s. St. Agatha is the patron saint of fire and
volcanic eruptions. She was put to death for refusing to
abandon her religious beliefs. In Poland there are many
traditions associated with the Feast of St. Agatha, including
the blessing of salt, bread, and water.

DIMINUTIVE: Agatka

FEAST DAY: February 5

***

Agnieszka. Agnes. Greek. "Pure, chaste."

St. Agnes is the patron saint of children and young girls. In
the 4ᵀᴴ century she was martyred (at age thirteen) for
refusing to deny God and marry a pagan. Popular in Poland
since the Middle Ages, this name has seen many variations
in spelling, including *Agneta* and *Jagnieszka*. It was given
to many Polish princesses from the Piast line, and to girls
born in small country villages.

DIMINUTIVES: Agunia, Jagunia, Agusia

FEAST DAY: January 21

***

Albina. Albina. German. Feminine form of **Albin**. "White."

DIMINUTIVE: None

FEAST DAYS: March 1, December 16

***

Aleksandra. Alexandra. Greek. Feminine form of
Aleksander. "Defender of men."
There are many saints named Alexander. The name has
appeared in Poland since the 14ᵀᴴ century and continues to
enjoy popularity.
DIMINUTIVES: Alka, Ala, Ola
FEAST DAYS: February 26, March 18, August 28

Anastazja. Anastasia. Greek. "Resurrection."
St. Anastasia was a noble woman who used her wealth to
aid Christians persecuted in Rome. Since the Middle Ages
the name has had various spellings, including *Anastazja*
and *Nastazyja*.
DIMINUTIVES: Nastka, Nastusia
FEAST DAY: December 24

Aniela. Angela. Greek. Feminine form of the Greek *Angelos*
and the Latin *Angelus*. "Angel."
This name became popular in the 18ᵀᴴ century primarily
through the Ursuline nuns. The founder of the order was
Angela Merici, who gathered twenty-eight women together
and named them the Ursulines in honor of St. Ursula.
DIMINUTIVE: Anielka
FEAST DAY: January 16

Anna. Ann. Hebrew. Derived from *Hannah*. "Grace."
According to Christian tradition, St. Anne was the mother

of Mary, mother of Jesus. She is the patron saint of childless women. According to a study in Cracow in 1989, it was the second most popular name after **Katarzyna** (Catherine).

DIMINUTIVES: Ania, Hania, Anka, Hanka
FEAST DAY: July 26

❖ ❖ ❖

Antonia, Antonina. Antonia. Latin. Feminine form of **Antoni** (Anthony). "Belonging to the Roman clan of Antonius."

Spelled *Antonija* in 1427.

DIMINUTIVES: Nina, Antosia, Tosia, Tośka
FEAST DAYS: May 3, June 13

❖ ❖ ❖

Apolonia. Apollonia. Greek. Feminine form of **Appoloniusz**. "Of the god Apollo."

St. Apolonia is the patron saint of dentists. In recent years, this name has been shortened to *Pola* and has become popular in the country. World renowned Polish-born actress Pola Negri was named Apolonia Chałupiec at birth.

DIMINUTIVES: Apolonka, Polonka
FEAST DAY: February 7

❖ ❖ ❖

Ariadna. Ariana. Greek. "Very pure, holy."

An uncommon name in Poland until recently.

DIMINUTIVE: None
FEAST DAY: June 7

❖ ❖ ❖

10

Augustyna. Augustina. Latin. Feminine form of **Augustyn** (Augustine). "Venerable."
In the past this name also appeared as *Jagustyna*. *Jagustynka* is the central female character in Władysław Reymont's Nobel Prize-winning book *Chłopi* (*The Peasants*).
DIMINUTIVES: Augustynka, Jagustynka
FEAST DAY: September 9

Barbara. Barbara. Greek. "Stranger, foreign."
St. Barbara is the patron saint of miners, architects, artillerymen and sailors. She died at the hands of her own father for refusing to deny her faith. She is invoked against lightning and an untimely death. Her feast day is celebrated by the miners of Poland with a special Mass and celebration. Favored since the 14TH century, numerous queens of Poland had this name.
DIMINUTIVES: Basia, Barbarka
FEAST DAY: December 4

Beata. Beata. Latin. "Fortunate, blessed."
A very popular name in previous centuries with various spellings, including *Biejta* (1392) and *Biata* (1458). Popular within the past twenty years.
DIMINUTIVE: Beatka
FEAST DAY: March 8

11

Benedykta. Benedicta. Latin. Feminine form of **Benedykt**
(Benedict). "Blessed."
Appeared in Polish documents as early as 1275. A quite
uncommon name today.
DIMINUTIVE: None
FEAST DAY: March 21

Bianka. Bianca. Italian. "White."
A name encountered in Polish literature, but never
became popular.
DIMINUTIVE: None
FEAST DAY: December 12

Blanka. Blanche. Spanish. "White, fair hair."
A more modern name to Poland.
DIMINUTIVE: None
FEAST DAYS: July 5, December 2

Bogdana. No English equivalent. Slavic. Feminine form of
Bogdan. Two-part name consisting of "god" + "given," or
"gift of God."
DIMINUTIVE: Bogna
FEAST DAY: February 6

Bogna. No English equivalent. Slavic. Feminine form of
Bogdan. Two-part name consisting of "god" + "given," or
"gift of God."

Many feel that this name is a diminutive of **Bogdana**, but it is also given independently as a first name.

DIMINUTIVE: None

FEAST DAYS: June 20, July 30

Bogumiła. No English equivalent. Slavic. Feminine form of **Bogumił**. Two-part name consisting of "god" + "dear," or "dear to God."

DIMINUTIVES: Bogusia, Boguśka, Bogunia

FEAST DAYS: June 10, December 20

Bolesława. No English equivalent. Feminine form of **Bolesław**. Two-part name consisting of "more, better" + "fame, glory, renown," or "he who can attain great glory."

DIMINUTIVE: None

FEAST DAY: August 19

Bożena. No English equivalent. Slavic. "Blessed by God." A very popular name in Poland. It is thought to be Czech in origin, and is sometimes spelled with two "n"s.

DIMINUTIVE: Bożenka

FEAST DAY: March 13

Bronisława. No English equivalent. Slavic. Feminine form of **Bronisław**. Two-part name consisting of "to protect" + "fame, glory, renown."

Blessed Bronisława was from the Opole region of Poland.

She had visions of Christ.

DIMINUTIVES: Bronia, Bronka, Brońcia

FEAST DAY: September 1

◈ ◈ ◈

Brygida. Bridget. Celtic. "Strength."

Appeared in Polish records as *Bryda* (1265) and as *Brygitta* (1465). The name became well-liked due to St. Bridget of Sweden who founded the Bridgettine Sisters.

DIMINUTIVE: Brygidka

FEAST DAY: July 23

Cecylia. Cecilia. Latin. "Blind."

St. Cecilia is the patron saint of church music and church musicians. Spelling appeared as *Cecylija* in 1265. A popular name in the 18TH century.

DIMINUTIVES: Cylka, Cyla

FEAST DAY: November 22

◈ ◈ ◈

Celestyna. Celestina. Latin. Feminine form of **Celestyn** (Celestine). "Heavenly."

DIMINUTIVES: Celestynka, Celka

FEAST DAY: April 6

◈ ◈ ◈

Celia, Celina. Selene, Selina. Latin. "Heaven."
Considered to be a shortened form of **Marcelina**. Celina
Szymanowska was the wife of Adam Mickiewicz
(1798–1855), Poland's most famous poet.
DIMINUTIVES: Cela, Celinka
FEAST DAY: October 21

❖ ❖ ❖

Czesława. No English equivalent. Feminine form of
Czesław (Ceslas). Two-part name consisting of "worship,
adoration" + "fame, glory, renown."
DIMINUTIVES: Cesia, Czeska
FEAST DAY: July 17

Danuta. Donna. Lithuanian. "God-given."
DIMINUTIVES: Danka, Danusia
FEAST DAY: June 24

❖ ❖ ❖

Delfina. Delphine, Duaphine. Greek. "Dolphin."
A name used by the French to designate the heir to the
throne of France. Considered an exceptionally beautiful
woman, Delfina Potocka (1807–1877) was thought to have
been the muse of such literary and musical greats as Juliusz
Słowacki, Zygmunt Krasiński, and Fryderyk Chopin.
DIMINUTIVE: None
FEAST DAY: December 12

❖ ❖ ❖

Dobrosława. No English equivalent. Slavic. Feminine form of **Dobrosław**. Two-part name consisting of "good" + "fame, glory, renown."
DIMINUTIVE: None
FEAST DAY: February 6

❖ ❖ ❖

Dominika. Dominica. Latin. Feminine form of **Dominik** (Dominic). "Of the Lord."
DIMINUTIVES: Domeczka, Dominiczka, Domka
FEAST DAYS: June 6, July 4

❖ ❖ ❖

Dorota. Dorothy. Greek. Feminine form of **Teodor** (Theodore). "God's gift."
St. Dorothy is the patron saint of brides, florists, and gardeners. In the Middle Ages, Dorothy was a popular name in Germany and among the Czechs. Its popularity slowly transferred to Poland, becoming especially favored in Cracow and remaining so today.
DIMINUTIVES: Dora, Dorotka
FEAST DAY: February 6

Edyta. Edith. Old English. "Happiness."

St. Edith took religious vows and spent her life caring for the sick (especially lepers) and the poor. This name is currently enjoying a revival in Poland.

DIMINUTIVE: Edytka

FEAST DAY: September 16

Eleonora. Eleanor. Origin unclear, but thought to be Greek. Derived from *Helen*. "Light."

Many English queens were named Eleanor, or a derivative thereof. Also the name of Polish Queen Eleanora Maria, wife of King Michael Wiśniowiecki (1640–1673) of Poland.

DIMINUTIVE: Eleonorka

FEAST DAYS: February 21, August 18

Eliza. Eliza. Hebrew. "Oath of God."

Shortened form of *Elizabeth*, but also used independently. Eliza Orzeszkowa (1841–1910) was a Polish writer and author.

DIMINUTIVE: None

FEAST DAYS: June 16, August 17, September 2

Elżbieta. Elizabeth. Hebrew. "Oath of God."

St. Elizabeth is the patron saint of pregnant women. In the Bible, Elizabeth was the wife of Zachary and mother of St. John the Baptist. A prominent name throughout the centuries, it appeared in Polish documents as *Elisabet* (1222) and *Elesbeth* (1307).

DIMINUTIVES: Ela, Elka, Elunia

FEAST DAY: November 5

❖ ❖ ❖

Emilia. Emily. Latin. Feminine form of **Emil**. "Of the clan of Aemilia."

A name favored by Polish queens and princesses. Maria Emilia was the daughter of Ziemowit, a Mazowian king who ruled that part of Poland. Popularized through Polish literature in the 18TH and 19TH centuries.

DIMINUTIVES: Emilcia, Emilka, Mila

FEAST DAYS: April 19, May 3, June 30

❖ ❖ ❖

Emma. Emma, Emmaline. Old German. "Great, lofty."

Appeared in Polish documents as early as 1265, and then more frequently in the 19TH century.

DIMINUTIVE: None

FEAST DAYS: April 8 & 19, June 24, November 24, December 3

❖ ❖ ❖

Eufemia. Euphemia. Greek. "Good prophecy" or "well spoken of."

Many Piast princesses were baptized with this name. An interesting variation is *Ofemija* (1399). A common name among the older generation.

DIMINUTIVE: None

FEAST DAYS: January 19, March 20, September 16

Eugenia. Eugenia. Greek. Feminine form of **Eugeniusz** (Eugene). "Of good descent."

DIMINUTIVES: Genia, Gieńka

FEAST DAYS: September 13 & 16

Ewa. Eve. Hebrew. "Giving life."

In the Bible, Eve was the wife of Adam and the mother of humankind.

DIMINUTIVES: Ewka, Ewunia

FEAST DAY: December 24

Felicja. Felice, Felicia. Latin. Feminine form of **Feliks** (Felix). "Happy, fortunate."

A well-known name in 18TH century Poland but no longer so. *Felicissima* ("the most happy") was another variation of this name in Poland.

DIMINUTIVES: Fela, Felcia, Felka

FEAST DAYS: January 24, April 27

Filomena. Philomena. Greek. "Friend, strength."
A name often taken by nuns when entering a religious order
or convent.
DIMINUTIVE: Fila
FEAST DAY: August 11

Flora. Flora. Latin. "Flower."
An extremely popular name in Europe at one time due to
Flora, the heroine in Sir Walter Scott's novel *Waverly*.
Today the name has lost its bloom.
DIMINUTIVES: Florka, Florynka
FEAST DAY: November 24

Florentyna. Florence. Latin. Feminine form of **Florentyn**.
"Flowering."
DIMINUTIVES: Florka, Florynka
FEAST DAY: June 6

Fortunata. Fortune. Latin. Feminine form of **Fortunat**
(Fortunatus). "Fortunate, lucky."
Encountered in the 18ᵀᴴ century and popular within
religious orders. Who didn't have a Sister Fortunata at least
once in their Catholic school education?
DIMINUTIVE: None
FEAST DAY: October 14

Franciszka. Frances. Latin. Feminine form of **Franciszek** (Francis). "Frenchman."

A well-liked name in 18ᵀᴴ century Poland. Gained popularity in the United States when Frances Xavier Cabrini became the first citizen of the United States to be canonized (1946). She established the first American convent and orphanage among Italian immigrants and is known as the patron saint of emigrants and migrants.

DIMINUTIVE: Frania

FEAST DAY: November 13

Genowefa. Genevieve, Jennifer. Origin either Celtic or Germanic. "Race of women."

St. Genevieve is the patron saint of Paris. A name that has grown in popularity in Poland since its origins in the 15ᵀᴴ century.

DIMINUTIVES: Genia, Gienka

FEAST DAY: January 3

Gertruda. Gertrude. Old German. "Spear, strength." Appeared in Poland in the Middle Ages. It was popular in the regions bordering Germany.

DIMINUTIVE: Gerta

FEAST DAY: November 16

Godzisława. No English equivalent. Slavic. Feminine
form of **Godzisław**. Two-part name consisting of "to join,
reconcile" + "fame, glory, renown."
DIMINUTIVE: None
FEAST DAY: December 24

Gościsława. No English equivalent. Slavic. Feminine form
of **Gościsław**. Two-part name consisting of "to entertain" +
"fame, glory, renown."
DIMINUTIVE: None
FEAST DAY: October 15

Grażyna. No English equivalent. Lithuanian. "Beautiful."
Popularized by Polish poet Adam Mickiewicz's 1823 poem
"Grażyna." An especially popular name before and after
World War II.
DIMINUTIVE: None
FEAST DAYS: April 1, July 26

Greta. Greta. Greek. Originally a German or Danish diminu-
tive of *Margaret*. "Pearl."
This particular spelling, along with *Grejta* (1384), was
common in Poland in the 14TH century. Later appeared as
Gryta and then disappeared from use in Poland altogether.
DIMINUTIVE: None
FEAST DAY: July 13

Grodzisława. No English equivalent. Slavic. Feminine form of **Grodzisław**. Two-part name consisting of "to build" + "fame, glory, renown."
DIMINUTIVE: None
FEAST DAY: October 12

Halina. Helene. Greek. Derived from *Helen*. "Bright one, shining one."
Many heroines in 19ᵀᴴ century Polish literature helped to bring this name to prominence.
DIMINUTIVES: Hala, Halka, Halinka
FEAST DAY: July 1

Helena. Helen. Greek. "Bright one, shining one."
In Greek mythology, Helen was the daughter of Zeus and the most beautiful of goddesses. She is Helen of Troy in Homer's *Iliad*. The name appears in Poland under a variety of guises, including *Elena* (1265) and *Alena* (1386). It was most popular during the 19ᵀᴴ century. Helena Modrzejewska (1840–1909) was a Polish-born actress of international fame.
DIMINUTIVES: Helcia, Hela
FEAST DAY: August 18

Hildegarda. Hildegarde. Old German. "Comrade in arms."
A name more frequently encountered in convents.
DIMINUTIVE: None
FEAST DAYS: April 30, September 17

Honorata. Honor. Latin. Feminine form of **Honorat**
(Honor). "Honor."
A popular name among country people and women taking
religious vows.
DIMINUTIVES: Honorcia, Honorka, Honoratka
FEAST DAY: January 16

Innocenta. Innocenta. Latin. Feminine form of **Innocenty**
(Innocent). "Innocent."
A name taken by many women upon professing their
religious vows.
DIMINUTIVE: None
FEAST DAY: July 28

Irena. Irene. Greek. "Peace."
St. Irene is the patron saint of peace. This name did not
appear in the Polish language until the 18ᵀᴴ century, but
afterward caught on very quickly.
DIMINUTIVES: Ira, Ircia, Irka
FEAST DAY: April 3

Iwona. Yvonne. Old German. Feminine form of **Iwo**
(Ives). "Yew."

A newer name in Poland, often shortened to *Iwa* and
pronounced like *Eva*.

DIMINUTIVE: Iwonka

FEAST DAYS: April 24, May 19 & 23

❖ ❖ ❖

Izabela. Isabella, Isabelle, Isabel, Isobel. Origin unclear,
but thought to come from the Spanish *Isabel* or the biblical
Jezabel. Possibly derived from *Elizabeth*. "Oath of God."
The name of many queens of Spain, its popularity spread
throughout Europe, including Poland. In 1519 King
Zygmunt I and his wife Queen Bona Sforza baptized their
first child Izabela, and this was the first time the name
appeared in Polish records. In the 17TH and 18TH centuries,
the name increased in popularity.

DIMINUTIVES: Iza, Izia, Bela

FEAST DAY: March 16

❖ ❖ ❖

Izydora. Isidora. Greek. Feminine form of **Izydor** (Isidore).
"Gift of Isis."

A name borrowed from the Greeks by the Romans and
then by the Christians. It gained popularity in the 18TH and
19TH centuries.

DIMINUTIVE: None

FEAST DAY: April 4

❖ ❖ ❖

Jadwiga. Hedwig, Heddy. German. "Safety in battle."
A name that traveled from Germany to Poland, possibly with
Hedwig of Meran (1174–1243), wife of King Henryk the
Bearded. After his death, she entered the convent at Trebnitz.
She was cannonized in 1243 and became the patron saint of
Silesia. Hedwig was also the name of the daughter of Louis
of Hungary, king of Poland from 1370–1382. Her marriage
to King Jagiello of Lithuania in 1385 united Poland with
Lithuania and made her queen of a vast empire.
DIMINUTIVES: Jadzia, Jaga, Iga
FEAST DAY: October 16

Janina. Jane. Hebrew. Feminine form of **Jan** (John). "The
Lord is gracious."
A name given in honor of the many saints named John. An
especially common name during the 1850s.
DIMINUTIVES: Janka, Janeczka
FEAST DAYS: June 24, December 27

Jaromira. No English equivalent. Slavic. Feminine
form of **Jaromir**. Two-part name consisting of "severe,
sharp" + "peace."
DIMINUTIVE: None
FEAST DAY: September 24

Jarosława. No English equivalent. Slavic. Feminine
form of **Jarosław**. Two-part name consisting of "severe,
sharp" + "fame, glory, renown."
DIMINUTIVE: None
FEAST DAY: January 21

Joanna. Joanne, Joanna, Joan. Latin. Feminine form of **Jan**
(John). "The Lord is gracious."
St. Joan of Arc is the heroine of France. As a young girl she
helped the King of France reconquer his country. She was
burned at the stake for heresy by her enemies. This name
can be counted among Poland's favorite girls' names. Many
interesting forms exist in Polish chronicles, including
Johanna (1265), *Jenna* (1275), and *Jena* (1372). The most
modern version appears as **Janina**.
DIMINUTIVES: Joasia, Jasia, Asia
FEAST DAY: May 30

Jolanta. Yolande. Greek. "Violet flower."
In early documentation, this name was spelled as *Jolenta*
(1277). Jolanta was also the name of a Polish princess who
was beatified in 1827. Gained popularity in later years due
to Iwaszkiewicz's central character of *Jola* in *The Maids
from Wilno*.
DIMINUTIVES: Jola, Jolka
FEAST DAY: June 15

27

Józefa. Josephine. Hebrew. Feminine form of **Józef**
(Joseph). "God will add."
A name given in honor of St. Joseph, foster father of Jesus
Christ and husband of Mary. It was popularized by
Josephine de Beauharnais (1763–1814), the first wife of
Napoleon. Throughout Europe, the name was especially
popular in small country villages.
DIMINUTIVES: Józia, Józka
FEAST DAY: March 19

Judyta. Judy, Judith. Hebrew. "To thank God" or "Jewess."
A very popular Polish name in the Middle Ages and among
Polish princesses, including the daughter of Bolesław
Krzywousty (Wrymouth) and the daughter of Mieszko III.
In the 19TH century it fell out of use and is now quite rare.
DIMINUTIVES: Judytka, Juta
FEAST DAYS: May 6, November 14, December 22

Julia. Julie, Julia. Feminine form of **Juliusz** (Julian).
"Downy, soft beard."
There were many saints with this name. St. Julia who lived
in Carthage, North Africa was murdered for refusing to
honor false gods. The name attained popularity in the
Western world through William Shakespeare's "Romeo and
Juliet." The play was first staged in Poland in 1799, and the
name became a favorite until World War II.
DIMINUTIVES: Julka, Julcia, Jula
FEAST DAYS: May 22, June 19, October 1

Justyna. Justina. Latin. "Just."

This name dates back to 14TH century Poland. It was most common in the 19TH century and was carried into the 20TH century by Polish literature.

DIMINUTIVE: Justynka

FEAST DAYS: April 14, September 26

Karina. Karen. Swedish. "Dear, beloved one."

A more modern name, appearing in Poland in the 20TH century. Also spelled *Karyna*.

DIMINUTIVES: Karynka, Karinka

FEAST DAYS: August 2, November 7

Karolina. Caroline. Old German. Feminine form of **Karol** (Charles). "Strong."

A popular name in 19TH century Poland, and currently enjoying a revival.

DIMINUTIVES: Karolinka, Karolcia, Karolka

FEAST DAY: November 4

Katarzyna. Catherine, Katherine. Greek. "Pure."

One of the most popular girls' names in Poland.

St. Catherine of Labouré, a French nun, gave the world the Miraculous Medal. On her feast day, unwed girls would

drop hot melted wax on water, study the shapes created by
the hardening wax, and then make marriage predictions.
For example, if the hardened wax resembled an axe or a
tree, the girl's future husband would be a forester. The same
ritual occurred on the Feast of St. Andrew on November 30.
The name was popularized by Catherine of Sienna, a
Dominican visionary.

DIMINUTIVES: Kasia, Kasienka

FEAST DAY: November 25

❖ ❖ ❖

Kinga. No English equivalent. Hungarian form of the Old
German **Kunegunda**.

This name came to Poland with Kinga (1224–1292),
daughter of Béla IV, King of Hungary, when she married
Polish King Boleslaus the Shy (1226–1279). She was also
the patron saint of the Poor Clares who had an abbey in
Stary Sącz in southern Poland.

DIMINUTIVES: Kinia, Kingusia

FEAST DAY: July 24

❖ ❖ ❖

Klara. Clara, Clare, Claire. Latin. "Bright, shining, clear."
This name, considered somewhat old-fashioned now,
was popular in Poland for centuries. St. Clare was the
13TH century founder of the Poor Clares, a Franciscan order
of nuns who serve the poor and needy.

DIMINUTIVES: Klarusia, Klarcia

FEAST DAY: August 11

❖ ❖ ❖

Klementyna. Clementine. Latin. Feminine form of
Klemens (Clement). "Merciful."
This name became popular in Poland during the 18TH century.
Maria Klementyna was the granddaughter of King Jan
Sobieski (1674–1696). Klementyna nee Tanska
Hoffmanowa (1798–1845) was a well-known Polish author
who wrote for women and children.
DIMINUTIVE: None
FEAST DAYS: September 9, November 23

Klotylda. Clotilda. Old German. "Famed in battle."
Now considered an old-fashioned name.
DIMINUTIVES: Klocia, Tylda
FEAST DAY: June 3

Konstancja. Constance. Latin. Feminine form of
Konstanty (Constantine). "Constant, steadfast."
A name given to many princesses and queens of Poland and
to members of the nobility during the Middle Ages.
DIMINUTIVES: Kostka, Kostusia
FEAST DAYS: January 18, March 11, July 17, September 19

Kordula. Cordelia. Origin unclear, but thought to be Latin.
"Little heart."
Appeared in 15TH century Poland, but was not a common name.
DIMINUTIVE: None
FEAST DAY: October 22

Kornelia. Cornelia. Latin. Feminine form of **Kornel**
(Cornelius). "Horn."

An uncommon name in earlier years, but today is gaining
popularity.

DIMINUTIVE: None

FEAST DAYS: February 2, March 31, September 16

Kryspina. Crispina. Latin. Feminine form of **Kryspin**
(Crispin). "Curly-haired."

DIMINUTIVE: None

FEAST DAY: October 25

Krystyna. Christine. Latin. "Belonging to Christ."

St. Christine was a martyr who was thrown into water with
a mill stone around her neck, but did not drown. The name
became more prominent as a result of Polish literature,
especially the works of Henryk Sienkiewicz. Appeared in
the 14TH century as *Kierstyna*.

DIMINUTIVE: Krysia

FEAST DAY: July 24

Kunegunda. See **Kinga**.

Laura. Laura. Latin. Shortened form of **Laurencja** (Lauren). "Laurel."

During the Middle Ages, this name appeared in Polish documents as *Laureta*.

DIMINUTIVE: None

FEAST DAY: June 17

Laurencja. Lauren. Latin. "Laurel."

DIMINUTIVE: None

FEAST DAY: December 18

Lawinia. Lavinia. Latin. Refers to Lavinium, an ancient town south of Rome.

A less common name in Poland.

DIMINUTIVE: None

FEAST DAY: April 14

Lea, Leja. Leah. Hebrew. "Cow."

A more common name among the Jewish population in Poland.

DIMINUTIVE: Lejka

FEAST DAY: April 22

Leokadia. No English equivalent. Greek. Feminine form of
Leokadiusz (Leocadius). "Cares about his people."
A prevalent name in the 19TH century and currently
regaining popularity. The name was translated to *Lydia* in
America, but this is not an accurate equivalent.
DIMINUTIVES: Loda, Lodzia, Leosia
FEAST DAY: December 9

Leonarda. Leonarda. Old German. Feminine form of
Leonard. Two-part name consisting of "lion" + "mighty."
DIMINUTIVE: None
FEAST DAYS: November 6 & 26

Lidia. Lydia. Greek. "Woman of Lydia."
Lydia was an ancient country in Asia Minor, now part of
northwest Turkey. A relatively new Polish name.
DIMINUTIVES: Lidka, Lidzia, Lideczka
FEAST DAY: March 27

Liliana. Lilian, Lillian. Latin. "Lily flower."
From ancient times, the lily has been a symbol of purity
and a favorite of flower names. The name honors the
Blessed Virgin, whose symbol is the white lily. In the
14TH century, the Old Polish spelling appeared as *Lilija*.
DIMINUTIVE: None
FEAST DAYS: September 4, December 8

Lubomiła. No English equivalent. Slavic. Feminine form of
Lubomił. Two-part name consisting of "loved" + "dear."
DIMINUTIVE: None
FEAST DAY: No known feast day

Lubomira. No English equivalent. Slavic. Feminine form of
Lubomir. Two-part name consisting of "loved" + "peace."
DIMINUTIVE: None
FEAST DAY: July 23

Lubosława. No English equivalent. Slavic. Feminine
form of **Lubosław**. Two-part name consisting of
"loved" + "fame, glory, renown."
DIMINUTIVE: None
FEAST DAYS: May 5, July 23

Lucyna. Lucia, Lucy. Latin. Feminine form of **Lucjan**
(Lucian). "Light."
A more common name in the 19TH century. St. Lucy was the
daughter of wealthy parents, but she gave away all of her
possessions to feed the poor.
DIMINUTIVES: Luca, Lucka, Lucynka
FEAST DAY: December 13

Ludmiła. No English equivalent. Slavic. Masculine
form is **Ludomił**. Two-part Czech name consisting of
"people" + "dear."

St. Ludmiła, patron saint of the Czechs, was the wife of
Boivoj, the first Czech prince to accept Christianity.
DIMINUTIVES: Ludka, Ludeczka
FEAST DAYS: February 20, May 7

Ludwika. Louisa. Old German. Feminine form of **Ludwik**
(Louis). "Renowned fighter."
St. Louise de Marillac (1591–1660) was the founder of the
Sisters (Daughters) of Charity, a religious order dedicated
to caring for the poor and providing them with hospital
care. A favorite name of long ago.
DIMINUTIVES: Ludka, Lusia
FEAST DAY: March 15

Ludwina. Ludwina. German. Roughly translated as "friend
of the people."
St. Ludwina (1380–1433) is the patron saint of the sick and
their caretakers.
DIMINUTIVES: Ludka, Ludwinka
FEAST DAY: April 14

Magda. A diminutive of **Magdalena**.
This shortened version became very popular in Poland.
DIMINUTIVES: Magdusia, Madzia
FEAST DAY: July 22

Magdalena. Magdalene, Magdalen. Hebrew. "Woman
of Magdala."
In the New Testament, Mary Magdalene is one of Jesus's
most devoted followers. She attended His burial and went
to annoint His body, only to find the tomb empty.
DIMINUTIVES: Magda, Madzia
FEAST DAY: July 22

Maja. May. Latin. Name associated with the month of May.
A newer name to Poland, thought to be a diminutive
of **Maria**.
DIMINUTIVE: Majka
FEAST DAYS: May 5, November 12

Małgorzata. Margaret, Marjorie, Margot. Greek. "Pearl."
This name appeared in 12TH and 13TH century Poland as
Margareta, *Margarita*, or *Margata* and in such shortened
variations as *Greta* (1352). The seventh most popular girls'
name in Poland in the 17TH century, it was less favored
in the 18TH century. It regained popularity in the 1960s
and 1970s.
DIMINUTIVES: Gosia, Małgośka
FEAST DAY: July 20

Malwina. Malwina. German. Two-part name consisting of
"court, justice" + "friend."
A name popularized by Polish literature.

DIMINUTIVE: Malwinka
FEAST DAY: July 4

❖ ❖ ❖

Marcelina. Marcellina. Latin. "Belonging to the clan of Marcellus."
A name associated with some of Poland's most notable women, including Marcelina nee Radziwiłł Czartoryski (1822–1857), a pianist and student of Chopin, and singer Marcelina Sembrich-Kochańska (1858–1935).
DIMINUTIVE: Marcelka
FEAST DAY: July 17

❖ ❖ ❖

Maria. Mary. Hebrew. "Wished-for child" or "rebellion."
As the name given to the mother of Jesus Christ, it was initially thought to be too sacred to use; but, Maria gradually became one of the most popular female names in the Christian world. In the 1700s, during the war with the Swedes, the Poles' attributed the successful defense of the shrine at Częstochowa to Mary. There are many feasts honoring the Blessed Virgin under various titles, and any one of these can be chosen as a personal feast day. One of the more popular choices is the Feast of the Assumption of Mary, designated here.
DIMINUTIVES: Maja, Marynia, Marysia
FEAST DAY: August 15

❖ ❖ ❖

Marianna. Marianne, Maryanne, Mary Ann. Hebrew. Feminine form of **Marian** (Marion). "Of the clan of Marius."
Derived from the Hebrew name **Maria**, this name also

38

appears as *Maryjenna* (1242) and *Maryjanna* (1243). It was especially well-liked in the 17ᵀᴴ and 18ᵀᴴ centuries—a time when the name *Maria* itself was rarely used.

DIMINUTIVE: None

FEAST DAYS: February 17, May 26, June 2, September 8

Marta. Martha. Aramaic. "Lady, mistress of the house." In the Bible, Martha was the sister of Mary and Lazarus, the latter of whom Jesus raised from the dead. She is the patron saint of housewives, which stems from her solicitude towards Jesus when He visited the family home. A favorite name during the period between World War I and World War II.

DIMINUTIVES: Marcia, Martunia

FEAST DAY: July 29

Martyna. Martina. Latin. Feminine form of **Marcin** (Martin). "Warlike."

DIMINUTIVE: None

FEAST DAY: January 30

Maryla. No English equivalent. Hebrew. Derived from **Maria**. Maryla Wereszczaki was the young love of Polish poet Adam Mickiewicz. Maryla Wolska (1873–1930) was a poet of modern Poland.

DIMINUTIVES: Marylka, Maryleczka

FEAST DAY: August 15

Maryna, **Marina**. Marina. Origin unclear, but thought to
   be Latin. Feminine form of **Marin**. "Of the sea, marine."
   DIMINUTIVE: Marynia
   FEAST DAY: March 3

Matylda. Matilda, Mathilda, Maude. Old German.
   "Powerful in battle."
   The oldest form of this name appeared as *Mathildis* (1035).
   Over the centuries there have been numerous variations,
   including *Metilidis* (1275), *Mecheldis* (1275), and
   Mechtilidis (1310).
   DIMINUTIVES: Tylda, Tyla
   FEAST DAY: March 3

Melania. Melanie. Greek. "Black, dark-skinned."
   A name more commonly found in America than in Poland.
   DIMINUTIVES: Mela, Melcia
   FEAST DAY: December 31

Melisa. Melissa. Greek. "Bee."
   A more modern name in Poland. The Lithuanian spelling
   is *Melita*.
   DIMINUTIVE: None
   FEAST DAYS: March 10, September 15

Michalina. Polish version of the French *Micheline*.
   Feminine form of **Michał** (Michael). "Who is like the Lord."

A relatively modern name in Poland.
DIMINUTIVE: None
FEAST DAY: September 29

❖ ❖ ❖

Mieczysława. No English equivalent. Slavic. Feminine
form of **Mieczysław**. Two-part name consisting of
"sword" + "fame, glory, renown."
DIMINUTIVE: None
FEAST DAY: January 1

❖ ❖ ❖

Mirosława. No English equivalent. Slavic. Feminine
form of **Mirosław**. Two-part name consisting of
"peace" + "fame, glory, renown."
DIMINUTIVES: Mira, Mirka, Mireczka
FEAST DAY: February 26

❖ ❖ ❖

Monika. Monica. Origin unclear, but thought to be Greek.
"Counselor."
St. Monica was the mother of St. Augustine, a brilliant
defender of the Christian faith. St. Monica helped her son
overcome a life of debauchery and self-indulgence. Only
somewhat popular in the 15TH century, this name gained
more of a following after World War II and again in the
1960s and 1970s.
DIMINUTIVE: Nika
FEAST DAY: August 27

❖ ❖ ❖

Nadzieja. Nadia, Hope. Slavic. "Hope."
This name is one of a trio of Sophie's daughters—Faith,
Hope and Charity—from Greco-Roman legends. The other
two names are not used in Poland.
DIMINUTIVES: Nada, Nadzia
FEAST DAY: September 30

❖ ❖ ❖

Natalia. Natalie. Latin. "Birthday of the Lord."
Appeared in Polish records in the 14TH and 15TH centuries.
DIMINUTIVES: Natalka, Talka, Tala
FEAST DAYS: July 27, August 26, December 1

❖ ❖ ❖

Nina. Shortened version of the Polish **Antonina** or **Janina**.
DIMINUTIVES: Ninka, Nineczka
FEAST DAYS: May 3, June 13

Oktawia. Octavia. Latin. "Eighth."
DIMINUTIVE: None
FEAST DAYS: March 16, August 6, November 20

❖ ❖ ❖

Olga. Olga. Russian form of the Scandinavian *Helga*. "Healthy, fortunate."

St. Olga was a Ruthenian princess and the wife of Prince Igor. *Alga* and *Holga* (1405) are Polish variations of this name. Olga Boznańska (1865–1940) is considered one of Poland's finest painters.

DIMINUTIVE: None

FEAST DAY: July 11

❖ ❖ ❖

Olimpia. Olympia. Greek. "One from Olympia."

DIMINUTIVE: None

FEAST DAYS: July 25, December 17

Paula. Paula. Feminine form of the Latin *Paulus*. "Small."

An uncommon name in Poland until recently.

DIMINUTIVE: None

FEAST DAY: January 26

❖ ❖ ❖

Paulina. Pauline. Feminine form of the Latin *Paulin*. "Belonging to Paul."

Appeared as *Pawlina* in 1369. Increased in popularity over the last twenty years.

DIMINUTIVE: Paulinka

FEAST DAY: June 22

❖ ❖ ❖

Pelagia. Pelagia. Greek. Feminine form of **Pelagiusz** (Pelagius). "Of the sea."
A common name in the 19ᵀᴴ century.
DIMINUTIVES: Pela, Pelunia
FEAST DAY: October 8

❖ ❖ ❖

Petronela. Petronella, Pernella. Latin. Feminine form of **Petroniusz** (Petronius). "Member of the clan of Petronia." An old-fashioned name, commonly found among older generation women and nuns.
DIMINUTIVE: Petronelka
FEAST DAY: May 31

❖ ❖ ❖

Prakseda. No English equivalent. From the Greek *Praxedes*. "Activity, action."
Appeared as *Praksa* in 1357. More common to the eastern border regions of Poland.
DIMINUTIVE: None
FEAST DAY: July 21

❖ ❖ ❖

Pryska. Priscilla. Latin. "Ancient, old, revered."
Rarely found in Polish sources.
DIMINUTIVE: None
FEAST DAY: January 18

❖ ❖ ❖

Przemysława. No English equivalent. Slavic. Feminine form of **Przemysław**. Two-part name consisting of "mind, thought" + "fame, glory, renown."

A rare name encountered initially in 1155–1156, and then infrequently throughout the centuries.

DIMINUTIVE: None

FEAST DAY: April 13

R

Rachela. Rachel. Hebrew. "Ewe."

In the Bible, Rachel was the wife of Jacob and mother of Joseph and Benjamin.

DIMINUTIVE: Rocha

FEAST DAY: September 30

Radosława. No English equivalent. Slavic. Feminine form of **Radosław**. Two-part name consisting of "glad" + "fame, glory, renown."

DIMINUTIVE: None

FEAST DAY: September 9

Rebeka. Rebecca, Rebekah. Hebrew. "A woman who takes a man's heart."

A common name among the Jewish population of Poland.

DIMINUTIVE: Rywka

FEAST DAY: March 9

Regina. Regina, Reyna, Queenie. Latin. "Queen."
A name given in honor of the Blessed Virgin Mary, Queen
of Heaven (*Regina Coeli*). A favorite name in the small
villages of southern Poland.
DIMINUTIVE: None
FEAST DAY: August 22

Renata. Renée. Feminine form of the Latin *Renatus*. "Reborn."
Cecylia Renata of France married King Władysław IV
(1595–1648) and became Queen of Poland, thus
popularizing the name.
DIMINUTIVES: Rena, Renatka, Renia
FEAST DAY: November 12

Roksana. Roxanne, Roxana. Persian. "Dawn, shining."
The name of the wife of Alexander the Great. A popular
name in Poland only within the past few decades.
DIMINUTIVE: None
FEAST DAYS: March 20, December 13

Romana. Ramona. Latin. Feminine form of **Roman**. "One
from Rome."
DIMINUTIVE: None
FEAST DAY: February 23

Róża. Rose. Latin. "Rose."
Popularized by St. Rose of Lima, the patron saint of Peru.

This name goes back in antiquity, but did not appear in Polish archives until 1470.
DIMINUTIVE: Rózia
FEAST DAY: August 23

Ruta. Ruth. Hebrew. "Friendship, friendly."
This name honors the heroine of the Book of Ruth in the Bible.
DIMINUTIVE: None
FEAST DAY: September 1

Sabina. Sabina. Latin. "Member of the Sabine Tribe."
The Sabines were a tribe in central Italy. In an effort to provide wives for the citizens of Rome, a mass kidnapping of the Sabine women was arranged. In literature this came to be known as the "Rape of the Sabine Women." St. Sabina was a wealthy Italian woman who was converted to Christianity by her slave, St. Seraphia. Both women were put to death for their faith in the 3RD century. A more common name today than in previous centuries.
DIMINUTIVE: Saba
FEAST DAY: August 9

Salomea. Salome, Salomea. Hebrew, from the word *shalom*.
"Peace."
Salomea was one of the women who ministered to Jesus.
The name appeared in Polish records as *Salome* (1146)
and *Salomeja* (1252). Given to many queens and princesses
of Poland, it was a popular name for girls until the
19TH century.
DIMINUTIVES: Sala, Salka, Salcia
FEAST DAY: November 19

Scholastyka. Scholastica. Latin. "Student, scholastic."
Scholastica was the much-loved twin sister of St. Benedict,
the founder of Western monasticism. She is considered the
patron saint of rain and is invoked against childhood
convulsions. This name is taken by many women entering
religious orders.
DIMINUTIVE: None
FEAST DAY: February 10

Serafina. Seraphina, Seraphine, Serafine. Hebrew. Feminine
form of **Serafin** (Seraphinus). "Flaming ones."
DIMINUTIVE: None
FEAST DAY: September 8

Seweryna. Severina. Latin. Feminine form of **Seweryn**
(Severin). "One from Severus."
A popular name in the 19TH century, but less so thereafter.

Diminutive: None
Feast Day: November 19

❖ ❖ ❖

Sławomira. No English equivalent. Slavic. Feminine form of **Sławomir**. Two-part name consisting of "fame, glory, renown" + "peace."
Diminutives: Sławka, Mira, Mirka
Feast Day: December 23

❖ ❖ ❖

Stanisława. No English equivalent. Slavic. Feminine form of **Stanisław** (Stanislas). Two-part name consisting of "become" + "fame, glory, renown."
A favorite Polish name for centuries, but less so today.
Diminutives: Stacha, Stasia, Staszka
Feast Days: May 8, August 14, November 13

❖ ❖ ❖

Stefania. Stephanie. Greek. Feminine form of **Stefan** (Stephen). "Crown."
St. Stephen was the first martyr of the church. He was stoned to death outside the walls of Jerusalem. In his memory, the people of Poland threw oats and wheat at their parish priest on his feast day. This name did not catch on in Poland until the 19TH century, when it began to appear in popular literature.
Diminutives: Stefa, Stefcia, Stefka
Feast Day: December 26

❖ ❖ ❖

Stela. Stella, Estelle, Estella. Latin. "Star."
Although definitely a feminine first name, it was also used
as a middle name for boys; Jan Stella Sawicki (1831–1911),
a Polish physician and writer, participated in the January
Uprising of 1863 against the Russians.
DIMINUTIVE: None
FEAST DAY: August 15

Stojanka. No English equivalent. Slavic. Feminine form of
Stojan. "Stand."
DIMINUTIVE: None
FEAST DAY: May 7

Świętosława. No English equivalent. Slavic. Feminine
form of **Świętosław**. Two-part name consisting of
"mighty" + "fame, glory, renown."
DIMINUTIVE: None
FEAST DAY: May 3

Tekla. Thekla, Thecla, Tecla. Greek. Two-part name
consisting of "god" + "fame, glory, renown."
A well-liked name dating back to the 12TH century, but is
now considered old-fashioned.
DIMINUTIVES: Teklunia, Teklusia
FEAST DAY: September 23

Teodora. Theodora. Greek. Feminine form of **Teodor** (Theodore). "God's gift."

This name appeared in 15TH and 18TH century Poland, then fell out of favor.

DIMINUTIVES: Teodosia, Dosia

FEAST DAYS: April 1, September 11

Teofila. Theophila. Greek. Feminine form of **Teofil** (Theophil). "Dear to God."

A more popular name in the 17TH century.

DIMINUTIVES: Teofilka, Tosia, Fila

FEAST DAY: December 28

Teresa. Teresa, Theresa. Origin unclear, but thought to be Greek. "Harvest, reap."

Due to the popularity of St. Teresa of Avila and St. Thérèse of Lisieux, this name has been very popular among Catholic families, including those in Poland.

DIMINUTIVES: Terenia, Tereska, Renia

FEAST DAYS: October 1 & 15

Tomisława. No English equivalent. Slavic. Feminine form of **Tomisław**. Two-part name consisting of "to torment" + "fame, glory, renown."

DIMINUTIVE: None

FEAST DAY: July 27

U

Urszula. Ursula, Ursuline, Orsula. Latin. "Little bear."
St. Ursula was a 4TH century martyr. In spite of the Ursuline
Order, the name was not especially popular in earlier
centuries. It was considered old-fashioned until the end of
World War II, when it began to increase in popularity.
DIMINUTIVES: Ula, Uleczka, Ulka
FEAST DAY: October 21

W

Wacława. No English equivalent. Slavic. Feminine form
of **Wacław** (Wenceslaus). Two-part name consisting of
"more" + "fame, glory, renown."
DIMINUTIVE: None
FEAST DAY: September 28

Walentyna. Valentina. Latin. Feminine form of **Walentyn**
(Valentine). "Mighty, valiant."
DIMINUTIVE: Wala
FEAST DAY: July 25

Waleria. Valerie, Valery, Valeria. Latin. Feminine form of
Walerian (Valerian). "Belonging to Valerius."

DIMINUTIVES: Wala, Walercia, Walerka
FEAST DAYS: April 28, June 5

❖ ❖ ❖

Wanda. Wanda. Origin unclear, but thought to be Slavic.
"The wanderer."
Some feel that this name derives from the Vandals, a
Germanic tribe. Found in some of Poland's earliest
chronicles, it became more widespread in the 17TH and
18TH centuries due to European literature.
DIMINUTIVES: Wandzia, Wandeczka, Wandusia
FEAST DAY: June 23

❖ ❖ ❖

Weronika. Veronica. Latin. "True image."
According to legend, a young woman named Veronica
wiped the face of Jesus on His way to the Crucifixion, and
an imprint of His features remained on the cloth. The
Polish pronunciation of this name sounds very similar to
the French *Véronique*.
DIMINUTIVES: Weronka, Wera, Werka
FEAST DAYS: January 13, February 4

❖ ❖ ❖

Wiesława. No English equivalent. Slavic. Feminine form of
Wiesław. Meaning unclear, but thought to come from an
old Russian two-part name consisting of "all" + "fame,
glory, renown."
DIMINUTIVES: Wiesia, Wieśka
FEAST DAYS: May 22, December 9

❖ ❖ ❖

53

Wiktoria. Victoria. Latin. Feminine form of **Wiktor**
(Victor). "Conqueror, victory."
While Polish records indicate the existence of this name in
the 13TH and 15TH centuries, it did not gain popularity until
the Victorian era, when many were naming their daughters
after England's Queen Victoria (1837–1901).
DIMINUTIVE: Wika
FEAST DAY: December 23

Wilhelmina. Wilhelmina, Willamina, Willa, Wilma.
Old German. Feminine form of **Wilhelm** (William).
"Strong fighter."
DIMINUTIVE: None
FEAST DAYS: May 26, October 25

Wiola. Viola, Violet. Latin. "Violet."
DIMINUTIVE: **Wioletta**
FEAST DAY: October 29

Wioletta. Violetta, Violette, Violet. Derived from the Italian
Violetta. "Violet."
A diminutive of **Wiola**. A well-liked name in Poland since
the 19TH century.
DIMINUTIVE: None
FEAST DAY: October 29

Wisława. No English equivalent. Slavic. Feminine form of
Wisław. Two-part name consisting of "lord" + "fame,
glory, renown."
DIMINUTIVE: Wisia
FEAST DAY: June 6

Władysława. No English equivalent. Slavic. Feminine form
of **Władysław**. Two-part name consisting of "to rule" +
"fame, glory, renown."
Like its male counterpart, this name was once very popular
but is now thought to be old-fashioned.
DIMINUTIVES: Włada, Władka, Władzia
FEAST DAYS: June 27, September 25

Włodzimiera. Vladimira. Slavic. Feminine form of
Włodzimierz (Vladimir). Two-part name consisting of "to
rule" + "peace."
DIMINUTIVE: None
FEAST DAYS: January 16, September 25

Wojciecha. Adalberta. Slavic. Feminine form of **Wojciech**
(Adalbert). Two-part name consisting of "warrior" + "joy."
DIMINUTIVE: None
FEAST DAY: April 23

Zdzisława. No English equivalent. Slavic. Feminine form
of **Zdzisław**. Two-part name consisting of "to lay down, set
down" + "fame, glory, renown."
Among the Czechs, Blessed Zdzisława is the patron saint of
young married couples and mothers.
DIMINUTIVES: Zdzisia, Zdziska
FEAST DAYS: January 29, November 28

Zenobia. Zenobia. Greek. Feminine form of **Zenobiusz**
(Zenobius). Two-part name consisting of "Zeus" + "life."
A common name among older generation Polish women.
DIMINUTIVES: Zena, Zenka, Zina
FEAST DAYS: February 20, December 24

Zenona. Zenona. Greek. Feminine form of **Zenon** (Zeno).
"Gift of Zeus."
DIMINUTIVES: Zena, Zenia, Zenka
FEAST DAY: June 23

Zofia. Sophia. Greek. "Wisdom."
This has always been one of the most popular girls' names
in Poland. The French form is *Sophie*.
DIMINUTIVES: Zosia, Zoska
FEAST DAY: May 15

Zuzanna. Suzanna, Susannah, Suzanne, Susan. Hebrew.
"Lily."

Various spellings in medieval Poland include *Ożanna*
(1265). Today, it is a name more commonly found in the
countryside.

DIMINUTIVES: Zuza, Zuzanka, Zuzka

FEAST DAYS: May 24, August 11

Zyta. Zita. Italian. "Little girl."

In Poland, St. Zyta is the patron saint of domestic workers.
Some feel that *Zyta* derives from the last part of the
name *Felicyta*.

DIMINUTIVE: None

FEAST DAY: April 27

BOYS' NAMES

Adam. Adam. Hebrew. "Man of the earth."

St. Adam is the patron saint of gardeners. In the Book of Genesis, Adam was the first man on earth created by God. The name appeared in Polish documents since the 12TH century. Adam Mickiewicz (1798–1855) was one of Poland's greatest poets; Adam Stefan Sapieha (1867–1951) was a bishop of Cracow.

DIMINUTIVE: Adasiek

FEAST DAY: December 24

Albin. Albin. Latin. "White."

Albin Dunajewski (1817–1894) was archbishop of Cracow and cardinal.

DIMINUTIVE: None

FEAST DAY: March 1

Aleksander. Alexander. Greek. "Defender of men."

A very popular name throughout the centuries. It was spelled *Aleksandr* and *Aleksender* during the 15TH century.

DIMINUTIVES: Alek, Olek

FEAST DAYS: March 18, August 28, December 1

❖ ❖ ❖

Aleksy. Alexis. Greek. "Defender and helper of men."

St. Alexis is the patron saint of wanderers and beggars. He was a Roman who lived as a hermit and devoted his life to good works. There were many miracles wrought in his name. Often considered a shortened form of **Aleksander**, the name appeared in Poland in the 14TH century.

DIMINUTIVE: Alek

FEAST DAY: July 17

❖ ❖ ❖

Andrzej. Andrew. Greek. "Manly."

St. Andrew is the patron saint of fishermen and spinsters. In the Bible, Andrew was one of the twelve apostles and a fisherman who followed John the Baptist. On the eve of his feast day, young unmarried girls would try to make predictions about their future husbands by dropping hot melted wax into a bowl filled with cold water; this caused the wax to form various shapes as it hardened. If the wax resembled a weapon or helmet, the young girl was thought to marry a soldier. In Poland, there were two versions of this name: *Andrzej* and *Jędrzej*. The former became the more popular version.

DIMINUTIVE: Andrzejek

FEAST DAY: November 30

❖ ❖ ❖

Antoni, **Antonin**, **Antoniusz**. Antony, Anthony. Latin.
"Belonging to the Roman clan of Antonius."
An extremely popular name in Poland throughout the
ages, chiefly due to St. Anthony of Padua, the patron saint
of lost or stolen articles. Its popularity began to fade in the
19TH century.
DIMINUTIVES: Antek, Antoś, Toni, Tosiek
FEAST DAY: June 13

Anzelm. Anselm, Ansel. Old German. Two-part name
consisting of "god" + "helmet."
Not a common name in Poland, but has appeared in
each century.
DIMINUTIVE: None
FEAST DAY: April 21

Appoloniusz. Apollonius. Greek. "Of the god Apollo."
DIMINUTIVE: Polek
FEAST DAY: April 18

Arkadiusz, **Arkady**. Arcadius. Greek. "Native of Arcadia."
DIMINUTIVE: Arek
FEAST DAY: January 12

Artur. Arthur. Celtic. "Bear."
A name that appeared in Poland in the beginning of
the 19TH century, and has become increasingly popular

since the 1970s. Artur Grottger (1837–1867) was a famous
Polish painter.

DIMINUTIVES: Artek, Artuś

FEAST DAY: October 6

August. Augustus. Latin. "Venerable."

An ancient name given to the eighth month of the
calendar, it was the name of many Polish kings: Zygmunt II
August (1520–1572), August II (1670–1733), August III
(1696–1763), and Stanisław August Poniatowski
(1732–1798).

DIMINUTIVES: Gustek, Gutek, Gucio

FEAST DAYS: May 7, August 3, October 31

Augustyn. Augustine, Augustin. Latin. "Venerable."

Also spelled *Jagustyn* in 1382.

DIMINUTIVE: Gustek

FEAST DAY: August 28

Bartłomiej. Bartholomew. Hebrew. "Farmer's son."

St. Bartholomew is the patron saint of beekeepers,
butchers, tanners, and cheese merchants. In the Bible,
Bartholomew was a disciple of Christ, one of the original
twelve apostles. The name was very popular in the Tatra

mountain region of Poland during the 16TH century. Often
appears in Polish folk songs and Christmas songs.
DIMINUTIVES: Bartek, Bartosz
FEAST DAY: August 24

Bazyli. Basil. Greek. "Kingly."
Appeared in old Polish documents as early as 1430. The
eastern Slavic version is *Wasyli* (1454).
DIMINUTIVE: None
FEAST DAY: June 14

Benedykt. Benedict. Latin. "Blessed."
This name arrived in Poland with the Benedictine monks
who followed the rule of St. Benedict. The name of
fifteen different popes, it was more popular in the past
than it is today.
DIMINUTIVES: Benek, Benio, Benuś
FEAST DAYS: January 12, February 12 & 21, March 31,
April 16

Bernard. Bernard. Old German. "Strong as a bear."
Popularized by the Cistercians who followed the rule of
St. Bernard of Clairvaux (1090–1153). St. Bernard is the
patron saint of beekeepers. Early forms of the name include
Biernat (1386), *Berhard* (1401), and *Barnard* (1433).
DIMINUTIVE: None
FEAST DAYS: May 20, August 20

Błażej. Blaise, Blase. Latin. "Stuttering."
St. Blaze is the patron saint of those who suffer from
diseases of the throat. On his feast day, the church holds a
special ceremony where throats are blessed. A very popular
name in small country villages.
DIMINUTIVES: Błażek, Błażko
FEAST DAY: February 3

Bogdan. No English equivalent. Slavic. Two-part name consisting of "god" + "given," or "gift of God."
An ancient Polish name with roots in the formative years of
the Polish state. There were a variety of spellings for this
name, but only two forms remained throughout the
centuries: *Bogdan* and *Bohdan*.
DIMINUTIVES: Bogdanek, Boguś
FEAST DAYS: March 19, July 17, August 31, October 2

Bogumił. No English equivalent. Slavic. Two-part name
consisting of "god" + "dear," or "dear to God."
A popular name today. The eastern Slavic spelling
is *Bohumil*.
DIMINUTIVE: Boguś
FEAST DAY: June 10

Bogusław. No English equivalent. Slavic. Two-part name consisting of "to God" + "fame, glory, renown," or "glory to God."
A very popular name during the Middle Ages, disappearing

in the 16TH century and reappearing the following century. Today, it remains among the most popular of Polish boys' names—so much so that the diminutive *Bogusz* has become an independent first name.

DIMINUTIVES: Boguś, Bogusz
FEAST DAYS: April 29, December 18

Bolesław. No English equivalent. Slavic. Two-part name consisting of "more, better" + "fame, glory, renown," or "he who can attain great glory."

A name tied to the Piast Dynasty which generated many kings of Poland. Absent for many years, it returned to popularity in the 19TH century with the resurgence of interest in Slavic names.

DIMINUTIVE: Bolek
FEAST DAY: August 19

Boniface. Boniface. Latin. "One of good fortune."

The name of nine popes. Appeared in old Polish documents as *Bonifacius* (1224) and *Bonefacy* (1258), but never became very popular.

DIMINUTIVE: None
FEAST DAY: May 14

Borys. Boris. Slavic. Derived from **Borysław**. "To fight."

A name common to Bulgarian czars, including Borys I, Christian ruler in the 9TH and 10TH centuries. In 1405 it was spelled *Borysz*.

DIMINUTIVE: None
FEAST DAY: May 2

❖ ❖ ❖

Borysław. No English equivalent. Slavic. Two-part name consisting of "fight, battle" + "fame, glory, renown." Also spelled *Borzysław* in 1220. Not a common name today.
DIMINUTIVES: Boleczek, Bolek, Boluś
FEAST DAY: June 19

❖ ❖ ❖

Bożydar. No English equivalent. Slavic. Two-part name consisting of "god" + "gift," or "gift of God." Not a common name today.
DIMINUTIVE: None
FEAST DAY: November 11

❖ ❖ ❖

Bożymir. No English equivalent. Slavic. Two-part name consisting of "god" + "peace."
DIMINUTIVE: None
FEAST DAY: January 4

❖ ❖ ❖

Bronisław. Bronislaus. Slavic. Two-part name consisting of "to protect" + "fame, glory, renown."
A name with origins in early Poland, and at one time a very popular name for boys. Less so today.
DIMINUTIVE: Bronek
FEAST DAY: September 1

❖ ❖ ❖

Budzisław. No English equivalent. Slavic. Two-part name consisting of "to awaken, arouse" + "fame, glory, renown." This name appeared in Polish documents dating from 1136.
DIMINUTIVE: None
FEAST DAY: December 2

C

Celestyn. Celestine, Celestina, Celeste. Latin. "Heavenly." The name of five popes, beginning with Celestine I in the 5TH century. Celestine V established the Celestine Order.
DIMINUTIVE: None
FEAST DAY: April 6

❖ ❖ ❖

Chrystian. Christian. Latin. "Christian."
Also spelled *Krystyjan* in the 13TH century. A common name in northern Poland.
DIMINUTIVE: None
FEAST DAY: June 12

❖ ❖ ❖

Chwalibóg. No English equivalent. Slavic. Two-part name consisting of "praise" + "god."
DIMINUTIVE: None
FEAST DAYS: January 24, February 28

❖ ❖ ❖

Chwalimir. No English equivalent. Slavic. Two-part name consisting of "praise" + "peace."
DIMINUTIVE: None
FEAST DAY: May 17

Cyprian. Cyprian. Latin. "Of Cyprus."
Not a common name, but has existed in every century.
Spelled *Cyprjan* in 1193. Cyprian Norwid (1821–1883)
was a Polish poet and playwright.
DIMINUTIVE: None
FEAST DAY: September 16

Cyryl. Cyril. Greek. "Lord."
A very popular name in the Balkans throughout the
centuries, gradually spreading to Poland. In the Bible, Cyril
was the brother of Methodius. Together, they were known
as the "Apostles of the Slavs."
DIMINUTIVE: None
FEAST DAYS: March 18, June 27

Czesław. Ceslas. Slavic. Two-part name consisting of
"worship, adoration" + "fame, glory, renown."
A very popular name due to Blessed Czesław, who is
reputed to have saved the city of Wrocław from the Tartars
in 1241. Appeared as *Czasław* in 1393.
DIMINUTIVES: Czesiek, Czesio, Cześ
FEAST DAY: July 17

Damian. Damian, Damien, Damon. Latin. "Of the people."
St. Damian is the patron saint of barbers, druggists and
chemical workers.
DIMINUTIVE: None
FEAST DAY: September 27

❖ ❖ ❖

Dawid. David. Hebrew. "Friend."
In the Bible, David slew Goliath. A popular name today.
DIMINUTIVE: None
FEAST DAYS: March 1, July 15, September 17, December 29

❖ ❖ ❖

Dobiesław. No English equivalent. Slavic. Two-part name
consisting of "brave, resourceful" + "fame, glory, renown."
DIMINUTIVE: None
FEAST DAY: May 13

❖ ❖ ❖

Dobrogost. No English equivalent. Slavic. Two-part name
consisting of "good" + "guest," or "good to guests,
hospitable."
A very ancient name that can be traced back to 1153.
DIMINUTIVE: None
FEAST DAY: July 14

❖ ❖ ❖

Dobrosław. No English equivalent. Slavic. Two-part name
consisting of "good" + "fame, glory, renown."
An uncommon name today.
DIMINUTIVE: None
FEAST DAY: January 10

Dominik. Dominic. Latin. "Of the Lord."
St. Dominic (1170–1221) was the founder of the
Dominican religious order. Dominicans established their
monasteries in Poland in the 13ᵀᴴ century. After a long
absence, this name is regaining popularity in Poland.
DIMINUTIVES: Domek, Domeczek
FEAST DAY: August 8

Edmund. Edmund. Old English. "Happy protector."
There were many Englishmen who became saints of the
church as priests and theologians. This name spread to
Poland, becoming popular in the 19ᵀᴴ century and in the
period between the two World Wars.
DIMINUTIVES: Mundek, Mundzio
FEAST DAYS: October 25, November 16 & 20

Eliasz. Elias, Elijah. Hebrew. "The Lord is my God."
Old Polish spellings include *Helijasz* (1212), *Elijasz*

(1406), *Ilijasz* (1430), and *Ilija* (1430). A popular variation in Russia and Lithuania is *Ilia*. Not a common name in Poland today.

DIMINUTIVE: None

FEAST DAY: July 20

Emil. Emil. Latin. "Of the clan of Aemilia."

Very popular in the 19TH century. Today, a common name among the older population.

DIMINUTIVE: Emilek

FEAST DAYS: March 19, May 22, June 25

Eugeniusz. Eugene. Greek. "Of good descent."

A well-liked name in Germany in the 18TH century, later spreading to Poland in the 19TH and 20TH centuries.

DIMINUTIVES: Gienek, Genio

FEAST DAYS: January 4, September 6, December 30

Fabian, **Pabian**. Fabian. Latin. "Of the Roman clan of Fabius."

Spelled *Pabijan* (1374) and *Fabijan* (1397) in old Polish records. This name was common in the Pomorze and Mazowsze regions of Poland, but declined in popularity in the 19TH century.

DIMINUTIVE: None
FEAST DAY: January 20

🔹 🔹 🔹

Felicjan. Felician. Latin. "Happy."
This name first appeared in Polish documents in 1499 and infrequently thereafter. It regained popularity in the 19TH century.
DIMINUTIVE: None
FEAST DAYS: January 24, June 9, October 29

🔹 🔹 🔹

Feliks. Felix. Latin. "Happy, fortunate."
The name of many popes throughout the history of Christianity. Very popular in the 16TH and 17TH centuries.
DIMINUTIVE: Felek
FEAST DAYS: July 21 & 27, November 20

🔹 🔹 🔹

Ferdynand. Ferdinand. Old German. Two-part name consisting of "peace" + "bravery."
A much-loved name in Spain and Portugal, and common to the Austrian Habsburgs: Ferdinand I, II, III. It spread to Poland in the 18TH and 19TH centuries.
DIMINUTIVES: Ferdek, Ferdzik
FEAST DAYS: May 30, June 3

🔹 🔹 🔹

Filip. Philip, Phillip. Greek. "Friend of horses, horse-lover."
One of the twelve apostles, this name became popular

throughout the Christian world. Appeared in 15TH century Polish documents as *Filip* and *Pilip*.

DIMINUTIVES: Fil, Filek

FEAST DAY: May 3

Florentyn. Florence. Latin. "Flowering."

A rare name in Poland, but has appeared as *Florentius* (1222) and *Florentinus* (1224).

DIMINUTIVE: None

FEAST DAYS: June 11, November 7

Florian. Florian. Latin. "Flowering."

St. Florian is the patron saint of brewers, chimney sweeps and soap boilers, and the protector of those in danger of fire and flood. The cult of St. Florian the Martyr increased in Poland at the end of the 12TH century when his relics were brought to Poland and laid to rest at the Wawel Cathedral in Cracow. Statues of this saint can be seen throughout Poland near rivers, lakes and bridges.

DIMINUTIVE: None

FEAST DAY: May 4

Fortunat. Fortunatus. Latin. "Fortunate, lucky."

A name often used in religious orders.

DIMINUTIVE: None

FEAST DAY: October 14

Franciszek. Francis. Latin. "Frenchman."

St. Francis is the patron saint of animals. This name was made popular by St. Francis of Assisi (1181–1226), founder of the Franciscan order of friars and lover of nature who gave the world the custom of the manger scene at Christmastime. He is one of the most popular saints of the Roman calendar, living a life of poverty and love and caring for the sick and needy. A very popular name in the 19TH century, and is common today among the older generation.

DIMINUTIVE: Franek

FEAST DAY: October 4

Fryderyk. Frederick, Frederic, Fredrick, Fredric. Old German. "Peaceful ruler."

Appeared in Polish documents at the beginning of the 12TH century. This name became especially popular in western Poland which borders Germany. Fryderyk Chopin (1810–1849) is Poland's most famous composer and pianist.

DIMINUTIVES: Fredyk, Fredzio

FEAST DAY: July 18

Gaweł. Gall, Gallus. Unclear origin, but thought to be Celtic. "Foreigner."

St. Gall, a 7TH century hermit, established the Benedictine monastery in Switzerland. Through the Benedictines, the name became popular among the Czechs as *Havel*. A well-liked name in Poland's Podhale region.

DIMINUTIVE: None

FEAST DAY: October 16

❖ ❖ ❖

Gerwazy. Gervase, Gervais. Unclear origin, but thought to be Greek. "To raise a voice in praise."

Common until the 15TH century, it was a name given to children born out of wedlock in the Ropczyce region of Poland.

DIMINUTIVE: None

FEAST DAY: October 12

❖ ❖ ❖

Godzisław. No English equivalent. Slavic. Two-part name consisting of "to join, reconcile" + "fame, glory, renown." Also spelled *Godzisz* (1204), *Godek* (1204), *Godka* (1243), and *Godosław* (1265).

DIMINUTIVES: Godek, Godko

FEAST DAYS: December 1 & 28

❖ ❖ ❖

Gościsław. No English equivalent. Slavic. Two-part name consisting of "to entertain" + "fame, glory, renown."
DIMINUTIVE: None
FEAST DAY: April 18

❖ ❖ ❖

Grodzisław. No English equivalent. Slavic. Two-part name consisting of "to build" + "fame, glory, renown."
DIMINUTIVE: None
FEAST DAY: October 12

❖ ❖ ❖

Grzegorz. Gregory. Greek. "Vigilant watchman."
St. Gregory is the patron saint of singers and students. The Feast of St. Gregory was traditionally celebrated on the day of his death, March 12, and was nearly a holiday for elementary grade pupils in Poland. A prominent name throughout the centuries, especially after World War II.
DIMINUTIVE: Grzesiek
FEAST DAY: March 12

❖ ❖ ❖

Gustaw. Gustav, Gustave. French form of the Swedish name *Göstaf*. "Staff of the gods."
Derived from *Augustus*, this name did not appear in Poland until the 19TH century. It was the name of a character in "Dziady," a very popular work by the Polish poet Mickiewicz.
DIMINUTIVES: Gustek, Gucio
FEAST DAY: August 2

❖ ❖ ❖

Gwalbert. Gualbert. German. "Splendid ruler."
In Polish records this name rarely appeared independently,
but rather was preceded by *Jan*, as *Jan Gwalbert*. St. John
Gualbert was an Italian saint who founded the Vallobrosan
Benedictines.
DIMINUTIVE: None
FEAST DAY: July 12

Henryk. Henry. Old German. "Ruler of the home."
St. Henry the Emperor founded monasteries and dioceses,
encouraged missionary activity, and lived an exemplary life
practicing the Gospel virtues. The name of many kings of
England, France, Germany and Poland, Henry became a
favorite boys' name in Europe.
DIMINUTIVE: Henio
FEAST DAY: July 15

Herbert. Herbert. Old German. Two-part name consisting of
"master" + "bright, shining."
A name with many spelling variations throughout the
centuries, including *Herbort* (1218), *Ebord* (1248),
Herbord (1255), and *Arbort* (1441). More common in areas
of strong German influence, such as Silesia.
DIMINUTIVES: Herbercik, Bercik
FEAST DAY: March 16

Hieronim. Jerome. Greek. "Sacred name."

St. Jerome translated the Bible into Latin and became the patron saint of librarians. Various spellings include *Jeronim* (1178) and *Jaronim* (1418). A popular name at the turn of the 20ᵀᴴ century.

DIMINUTIVE: Hirek

FEAST DAY: September 3

Hipolit. Hippolytus. Greek. "One who frees horses."

This name originates from Greek mythology. Also spelled *Ipolit* (1244) and *Polit* (1424).

DIMINUTIVES: Hipcio, Hipek

FEAST DAY: August 13

Honorat. Honor. Latin. "Honor."

DIMINUTIVE: None

FEAST DAYS: January 16, February 8

Hubert. Hubert. Old German. Two-part name consisting of "mind" + "bright, brilliant."

St. Hubert is the patron saint of hunters.

DIMINUTIVE: None

FEAST DAY: November 3

Idzi. Giles, Gyles. Greek. "Aegis, shield of Zeus."
According to tradition, St. Giles is the patron saint of
nursing mothers. Many churches in Cracow and Wrocław
are named after this saint. In 1186, the name appeared as
Egidus, similar to the Latin *Egidua*. This name has
survived throughout the centuries, but is rarely seen today.
DIMINUTIVES: Idzik, Jidzik
FEAST DAYS: April 23, September 1

Ignacy. Ignatius. Latin. "Fiery one."
When the Jesuits brought the cult of St. Ignatius Loyola
(1491–1556) to Poland and established their order, this
name became widespread.
DIMINUTIVE: Ignacek
FEAST DAY: July 31

Igor. Igor. Russian. Possibly derived from the Scandinavian
Ingvarr. "To protect, defend."
Not a common name in Poland.
DIMINUTIVES: Igorek, Iguś
FEAST DAY: October 1

Inocenty. Innocent. Latin. "Innocent."
Thirteen popes have taken this name throughout the centuries.
DIMINUTIVE: None
FEAST DAYS: April 17, June 22, July 28, August 13

Iwo, Iwon. Ives. Old German. "Yew."
The patron saint of lawyers, St. Ives was a priest, pastor, lawyer, and judge. He spent his life caring for the sick, feeding the hungry, and ministering to the poor. This name is not common in English-speaking countries, but enjoys immense popularity in Poland and in other Slavic countries.
DIMINUTIVE: None
FEAST DAY: May 19

Izajasz. Isaiah. Hebrew. "The Lord is generous."
Name of the prophet Isaiah. Blessed Isaiah Bonner was born in Cracow, joined the Augustine Order, and tended to the sick. Also spelled *Jezajasz* (1250), *Izajasz* (1258), and *Ezajasz* (1421).
DIMINUTIVE: None
FEAST DAYS: February 16, July 6

Izydor. Isidore. Greek. "Gift of Isis."
Isidore of Spain worked as a laborer, but devoted his entire life to prayer. As a result, he is called the patron saint of

farmers and farm laborers. A well-liked name among
Greeks, Romans, and Christians.
DIMINUTIVES: Izydorek, Dorek
FEAST DAY: May 10

Jacek. Hyacinth. Greek. "Hyacinth."
In Greek mythology, flowers were said to have sprung
from the blood of Hyacinthus, a Greek youth accidentally
killed by Apollo. Thus, the hyacinth flower was named.
St. Hyacinth (*c*. 1200–1257) was one of the first saints of
Poland. He was a Dominican who founded the first
Dominican monastery in Poland. A favorite name in the
18TH and 20TH centuries.
DIMINUTIVE: Jacuś
FEAST DAY: August 17

Jakub. Jacob. Hebrew. "He who supplants."
The English variant of Jacob is James. St. James the
Apostle was a fisherman. He and his brother were mending
nets when Jesus called to them: "Come, follow me." A pop-
ular boys' name throughout the centuries.
DIMINUTIVES: Kuba, Kubuś, Jakubek
FEAST DAY: July 25

Jan. John. Hebrew. "The Lord is gracious."
In the Bible, John the Baptist began preaching in the
wilderness of Judea, and he baptized his followers
in the River Jordan. A very popular boys' name in
Poland throughout the centuries; between the 14ᵀᴴ and
15ᵀᴴ centuries, every eighth male in Cracow was named
John. In 1978, Cardinal Karol Wojtyła took the name John
Paul II when he became pope of the Catholic Church.
DIMINUTIVES: Janek, Jasiek
FEAST DAY: June 24

Jaromir. No English equivalent. Slavic. Two-part name
consisting of "severe, sharp" + "peace."
Although it appeared in Polish documents (1287), this
name was more popular among eastern Slavs.
DIMINUTIVE: None
FEAST DAY: September 24

Jarosław. No English equivalent. Slavic. Two-part name
consisting of "severe, sharp" + "fame, glory, renown."
DIMINUTIVES: Jarek, Jareczek
FEAST DAY: January 21

Jerzy. George. Greek. "A farmer, one who tills the soil."
St. George is the patron saint of England, knights,
armorers, and archers. A knight and slayer of dragons,
he had a large following during the Middle Ages. A

much-loved name in Poland, it was equally favored in
Czechoslovakia, Germany, Lithuania, and Russia.
DIMINUTIVES: Jerzyk, Jurek
FEAST DAY: April 23

Joachim. Joachim. Hebrew. "The Lord exalts."
St. Joachim was the husband of St. Anne and the father of
the Blessed Virgin Mary. Other spelling variations of this
name included *Jachym* (1388), *Jochym* (1397), *Ofim*
(1419), and *Achym* (1464).
DIMINUTIVE: Joachinek
FEAST DAY: August 16

Jozafat, **Józefat**. Josephat. Hebrew. "The Lord judges."
In Poland, this name was made popular by St. Jozephat Jan
Kuniewicz (1580–1632). Józefat Ignacy Łukaszewicz
(1789–1850) was a famous Polish painter.
DIMINUTIVE: None
FEAST DAY: November 12

Józef. Joseph. Hebrew. "God will add."
In the Bible, Joseph is the son of Jacob and Rachel, the
husband of the Blessed Virgin Mary, and the foster father of
Jesus. Throughout the centuries, this name has appeared in
various forms without the diacritical mark above the letter
"o": *Jozef* (1234), *Jesyp* (1491), and *Josyf* (1498). It was
the most popular boys' name in 18TH and 19TH century

Poland. The cult of St. Joseph was popularized by the Bernadine monks and the Jesuits.

DIMINUTIVES: Józefek, Józek

FEAST DAY: March 19

Juliusz. Julian. Latin. "Downy, soft beard."

Pope St. Julius I worked diligently to defend the Catholic faith against heretics in the 4TH century. A well-liked boys' name in Poland. One of Poland's most famous romantic poets was Juliusz Słowacki; Juliusz Kossak was an outstanding Polish painter.

DIMINUTIVE: Julek

FEAST DAY: April 12

Justyn. Justin. Latin. "Just, fair."

Never a very popular Polish name, except among those taking religious vows.

DIMINUTIVE: None

FEAST DAYS: January 4, June 1, July 14, October 30

Kacper, **Kasper**. Casper, Jasper. Unclear origin, but
thought to be Persian. "Bearer or keeper of the treasure."
According to tradition, Casper is one of the Three Kings,
along with **Melchior** and Balthazar. The form *Kacper* is
commonly found in small country villages. Other variations
included *Kaspar* (1375) and *Gaspar* (1391).
DIMINUTIVES: Kasparek, Kacperek, Kaspruś
FEAST DAY: January 6

Kajetan. Cajetanus. Latin. "One who comes from the town
of Caieta."
This name appeared in Polish documents in the 18TH century
and spread due to the works of St. Cajetan (1450–1547).
St. Cajetan was the founder of the Theatines, a congregation
of reformed priests who assisted in the Catholic Reforma-
tion. He was canonized in the 17TH century. Not a popular
name today.
DIMINUTIVE: None
FEAST DAY: August 7

Kanimir. No English equivalent. Slavic. Two-part name
consisting of "to invite" + "peace."
DIMINUTIVE: None
FEAST DAY: June 9

Karol. Charles. Old German. "Strong."

St. Charles is the patron saint of apple orchards and seminarians. A very old German name which spread throughout Europe largely due to Charlemagne (742–814). The Polish version derives from the Latin *Carolus*.

DIMINUTIVES: Karolek, Lolek
FEAST DAY: November 4

Kazimierz. Casimir. Slavic. "Bringing peace."

St. Casimir is the patron saint of Poland and Lithuania. Two major Polish figures contributed to the popularity of this name: the first was Polish King Kazimierz the Great (1310–1370), who brought peace and prosperity to Poland after many years of strife; the second was St. Kazimierz (1458–1484), a Polish prince who devoted his short life to prayer and love of the poor. When St. Kazimierz died at the age of twenty-six, many miracles were said to have occurred at his tomb. He was canonized in 1521.

DIMINUTIVE: Kazik
FEAST DAY: March 4

Klemens. Clement. Latin. "Merciful."

Clement was the third pope after St. Peter to rule the Church, and he is honored as a martyr. A favorite boys' name in Poland throughout the centuries, it had various spellings including *Klement* (1311) and *Kliment* (1411).

DIMINUTIVE: Klimko
FEAST DAY: November 23

Konrad. Conrad. Old German. "Courageous advice."
A very popular name in Germany during the Middle Ages
and eventually was brought to Poland. The name of many
kings of Mazowsze and Silesia.
DIMINUTIVE: None
FEAST DAY: February 19

❖ ❖ ❖

Konstanty. Constantine. Latin. "Constant, steadfast."
St. Constantine was a Cornish prince who relinquished his
crown to become a monk. In the 13TH and 14TH centuries,
this name was popular in the eastern regions of Poland,
likely due to the influence of Roman Emperor Constantine
the Great (274–337).
DIMINUTIVE: Kostek
FEAST DAY: March 11

❖ ❖ ❖

Kornel. Cornelius. Latin. "Horn."
This name appeared in 15TH century Polish documents as
the Latin form, *Cornelius*.
DIMINUTIVE: None
FEAST DAY: September 16

❖ ❖ ❖

Kosma. Cosmo. Greek. "Order, form."
The twin Arab brothers, Cosmas and Damian, were
legendary physicians in ancient Syria. During the Middle
Ages, they were the patron saints of physicians and
druggists.

DIMINUTIVE: None
FEAST DAY: September 27

Kryspin. Crispin. Latin. "Curly-haired."
St. Krispin is the patron saint of tailors, saddlemakers, and tanners. Spelled *Krzyszpin* during the 13TH century.
DIMINUTIVE: None
FEAST DAY: October 25

Krystian. Christian. Latin. "Christian."
This name was spelled *Krystyjan* and *Chrystian* during the 13TH century.
DIMINUTIVE: None
FEAST DAY: December 4

Krystyn. No English equivalent. Derived from the Latin *Christinus*. "Belonging to Christ."
DIMINUTIVE: None
FEAST DAYS: July 26, November 12, December 4

Krzesisław. No English equivalent. Slavic. Two-part name consisting of "to arouse, stir" + "fame, glory, renown."
DIMINUTIVE: None
FEAST DAY: September 11

Krzysztof. Christopher. Greek. "One who carries Christ."
St. Christopher is the patron saint of bachelors, horsemen,

travelers, and police officers. One of the most popular boys' names in Poland, dating from World War I to the present.
DIMINUTIVES: Kryzyś, Krzysiek
FEAST DAY: July 25

Ksawery. Xavier. Spanish. "One from Navarre."
The region of Navarre between France and Spain was the birthplace of St. Francis Xavier (1506–1552). Together with St. Ignatius Loyola he founded the Society of Jesus, a religious order dedicated to education. A well-liked name in Poland, often given as *Francis Xavier*. Franciszek Ksawery Malinowski (1808–1881) was a notable priest and linguist from the Pozań region.
DIMINUTIVE: None
FEAST DAY: December 3

L

Laurencjusz. Laurence, Lawrence. Latin. "One from Laurentum."
Although it appeared in various forms, including *Laurentius* (1203) and *Loranc* (1399), the name *Wawrzyniec* was preferred.
DIMINUTIVES: Lorko, Lorek
FEAST DAY: August 10

Lech. No English equivalent. Origin and meaning unclear, but thought to derive from the Slavic *Leszek*.

Lech was the legendary founder of Poland and the brother of Rus and Czech. An uncommon name in the past but has gained popularity due to Lech Wałęsa, founder of the Solidarity Movement, president of Poland, and 1990 Nobel Peace Prize winner.

Diminutive: None

Feast Day: August 12

Leo, **Leon**. Leo, Leon. Greek. "Lion."

This name appeared as *Leo* (1265) and *Leon* (1443) in Polish archives, with both forms favored until the 17TH century. Thirteen popes were named *Leo*. Over time, *Leon* became the name of choice. During the Middle Ages, the form **Lew** was also used.

Diminutive: Leonek

Feast Days: April 11, 19 & 22, June 12 & 28, and numerous others

Leokadiusz. Leocadius. Greek. "Cares about his people."

Not a common name in Poland.

Diminutive: None

Feast Day: December 9

Leonard. Leonard. Old German. Two-part name consisting of "lion" + "mighty."

St. Leonard is the patron saint of prisoners, the mentally ill, and birthing mothers. He was a Frankish lord who spent

much of his life working among captives and prisoners.
The cult of St. Leonard (6ᵀᴴ century) was spread by the
Cistercian monks. The name appeared in Polish documents
as *Leonard* (1193), and later as *Lenart* and *Lenhart* (1399).
Especially popular in the Podlesie and Maszowsze regions
of Poland, as well as in Lithuania.

DIMINUTIVE: None

FEAST DAY: November 6

Leopold. Leopold. Old German. "Bold among the people."
A common name in Austria, since St. Leopold is the patron
saint of Lower Austria. Not a very popular name in Poland,
but has resurfaced in recent years.

DIMINUTIVES: Poldek, Poldzio

FEAST DAY: November 15

Leszek. Les. Slavic. "To act cunningly."
Polish etymologists are unsure as to the precise origin
of this name, knowing only that it appeared in Polish
documents in various forms in the 12ᵀᴴ and 13ᵀᴴ centuries.
Possibly derived from the ancient name **Lech**.

DIMINUTIVE: Lesio

FEAST DAY: June 3

Lew. No English equivalent. Slavic version of the Greek
Leo. "Lion."
A name with possible origins in Russia, but also found
among Poland's most notable historic figures; Lew Sapieha

(1557–1633) was the Grand Field Marshal of Lithuania and the advisor to King Zygmunt III Waza (1566–1632).
DIMINUTIVE: None
FEAST DAY: May 11

❖ ❖ ❖

Longin. Longin. Latin. "Long."
This name derives from St. Longin, a Roman legionnaire who was said to have pierced the side of Christ at the Crucifixion. He later converted and died a martyr's death. In Poland, his name was popularized by one of the heroes in Henryk Sienkiewicz's *With Fire and Sword*.
DIMINUTIVE: None
FEAST DAY: March 15

❖ ❖ ❖

Lubomił. No English equivalent. Slavic. Two-part name consisting of "loved" + "dear."
DIMINUTIVE: None
FEAST DAY: No known feast day

❖ ❖ ❖

Lubomir. No English equivalent. Slavic. Two-part name consisting of "loved" + "peace."
A common name in Czechoslovakia, often spelled *Lubomer*. Gave rise to the surname *Lubomirski*.
DIMINUTIVE: None
FEAST DAYS: March 21, July 31

❖ ❖ ❖

Luborad. No English equivalent. Slavic. Two-part name consisting of "loved" + "help."
DIMINUTIVE: None
FEAST DAY: December 22

Lubosław. No English equivalent. Slavic. Two-part name consisting of "loved" + "fame, glory, renown."
DIMINUTIVE: None
FEAST DAYS: May 5, July 23

Lucjan. Lucian. Latin. "Light."
An unusual and rare form of the name *Lucius*. Not popular in Poland until the 19ᵀᴴ and 20ᵀᴴ centuries.
DIMINUTIVE: Lucek
FEAST DAYS: January 7, February 11, June 13

Ludomił. No English equivalent. Slavic. Two-part name consisting of "people" + "dear."
DIMINUTIVE: None
FEAST DAY: February 20

Ludomir. No English equivalent. Slavic. Two-part name consisting of "people" + "peace."
DIMINUTIVE: Ludek
FEAST DAY: November 10

Ludwik. Louis, Lewis. Old German. "Renowned fighter."
Louis the Great of Hungary (1326–1382) was the ruler of
Poland from 1370 until his death. However, the name gained
prominence with Louis XIV (1643–1715), King of France.
DIMINUTIVE: Ludek
FEAST DAY: August 25

Łukasz. Lucas, Luke. Latin. "From Lucanus."
St. Luke the Evangelist, author of the third Gospel, was a
Greek doctor. He is considered the patron saint of artists
and doctors. While this name appeared in old Polish
archives, it has gained the most popularity within the last
twenty-five years.
DIMINUTIVE: Łukaszek
FEAST DAY: October 18

Maciej. Matthias. Hebrew. "Gift of the Lord."
A highly popular name in Poland since ancient times.
Especially well-liked in the small mountain villages of
Podhale. A common name for male characters in Poland's
finest works of literature.
DIMINUTIVE: Maciek
FEAST DAYS: January 30, February 24, May 14

Maksymilian. Maximilian. Latin. "Greatest."

Maximilian Kolbe was a Franciscan priest who offered his life in place of that of a younger man with a family at the Nazi concentration camp of Auschwitz. He died in 1941 and was canonized in 1982.

DIMINUTIVES: Maks, Maksymek

FEAST DAY: August 14

❖ ❖ ❖

Malachiasz. Malachi. Hebrew. "My messenger."

DIMINUTIVE: None

FEAST DAYS: January 14, November 3

❖ ❖ ❖

Manfred. Manfred. Old German. "Man of peace."

A more common name in Silesia, in western Poland.

DIMINUTIVE: None

FEAST DAY: October 4

❖ ❖ ❖

Marceli. Marcellus. "One from the clan of Marcellus."

The Latin *Marcellus* first appeared in Polish documents in 1065, and later found favor in the shortened *Marceli* and *Marcel*. It was most popular in the 19TH century and the beginning of the 20TH century.

DIMINUTIVE: Marcyś

FEAST DAY: January 16

❖ ❖ ❖

Marcin. Martin, Martyn. Latin. "Warlike."

The patron saint of beggars, wine growers and innkeepers, St. Martin of Tours is one of the most popular saints of

France. There are many legends surrounding him, including one where he meets a naked man, gives him his coat and soon afterwards has a vision in which Christ is wearing the coat. A popular name in Poland after World War II, but was given to some of Poland's finest scholars, authors, and historians throughout history.

DIMINUTIVE: Marcinek

FEAST DAY: November 11

Marek. Marcus, Mark, Marc. Latin. "Warlike."
St. Mark is the patron saint of writers, notaries, basketmakers, and glassmakers. The name dates back to ancient Rome with Marcus Aurelius and Emperor Marcus Tulius Cicero. It became a Christian name through St. Mark, the author of the Gospel according to Mark. His symbol was the lion.

DIMINUTIVE: Mareczek

FEAST DAY: April 25

Marian. Marion. Latin. "Of the clan of Marius."
While many female names are derived from masculine names, this male name comes from the feminine **Maria**. It gained popularity in Poland in the latter part of the 20TH century.

DIMINUTIVES: Marianek, Maniek, Maruś

FEAST DAYS: April 20, May 6

Marin. Marin. Latin. "Of the sea, marine."
This name is sometimes spelled *Maryn*.
DIMINUTIVE: None
FEAST DAYS: March 8, December 15

Mariusz. Marius. Latin. "Of the clan of Marius."
Counted among Poland's most popular boys' names
following World War II.
DIMINUTIVE: Mariuszek
FEAST DAY: January 19

Mateusz. Matthew. Hebrew. "Gift of the Lord."
St. Matthew is the patron saint of tax collectors and
customs officers. The apostle Matthew wrote the first book
of the New Testament. A cherished name in Podhale, the
southern mountain region of Poland.
DIMINUTIVES: Maciek, Mateuszek
FEAST DAY: September 21

Maurycjusz, **Maurycy**. Maurice, Morris. Latin. "Moor,
belonging to Maurus."
The patron saint of the Papal Swiss Guard. It is believed
that St. Maurice (3RD century) died in Switzerland at
Agaunum, which today is called St. Moritz/St. Maurice in
his memory. A popular name throughout the 19TH century.
DIMINUTIVE: None
FEAST DAY: September 22

Medard. Medard. German. Two-part name consisting of "might" + "brave."

St. Medard was the patron saint of farmers, gardeners, and brewers during the Middle Ages.

DIMINUTIVE: None

FEAST DAY: June 8

Melchior. Melchior. Hebrew. "God is my light."

According to tradition, Melchior was one of the Three Kings along with Casper and Balthazar. A popular name throughout the Middle Ages, it had a variety of spellings, including *Malchior* (1450) and *Melcher* (1476).

DIMINUTIVE: None

FEAST DAY: January 6

Metody. Methodius. Greek. "Method."

A well-known name among southern and eastern Slavs, comemorating two saints—St. Cyril and St. Methodius— who brought them Christianity.

DIMINUTIVE: None

FEAST DAYS: February 14, May 11

Michał. Michael. Hebrew. "Who is like the Lord."

In the Bible, Michael the archangel led the heavenly army against the forces of evil and became the patron saint of Christian warriors. In the Middle Ages, St. Michael was the patron saint of knights, and the leading name

for boys during this time. Other spellings included *Michal* (1220), *Michial* (1394), and *Mechel* (1441). Also a popular name in Russian territories.

DIMINUTIVE: Misiek

FEAST DAY: September 29

◈ ◈ ◈

Mieczysław. No English equivalent. Slavic. Two-part name consisting of "sword" + "fame, glory, renown."

Polish chroniclers feel that this was the full name of Mieszko I, the first king of Poland. During the 19TH century, Polish kings began using this full name.

DIMINUTIVES: Miecio, Mieczyk, Mietek

FEAST DAY: January 1

◈ ◈ ◈

Mieszko. No English equivalent. Slavic. Shortened version of **Mieczysław**.

Mieszko I was the founder of the Piast Dynasty.

DIMINUTIVE: None

FEAST DAY: January 1

◈ ◈ ◈

Mikołaj. Nicholas, Nicolas. Greek. "Victorious people."

The patron saint of Russia. According to Polish documents, the name appeared as *Nicolaus* in the 12TH century, and as *Nichol* and *Mikołojek* in the 13TH and 14TH centuries. St. Nicholas is one of the most popular saints in Christendom. The name became dear through the legendary Saint Nicholas, Bishop of Myra and patron saint of little children,

young maidens, schoolboys, bakers, and others. His feast
day was considered a special holiday by shepherds and a
day of protection against wild animals, especially wolves.

DIMINUTIVE: Mikołajek

FEAST DAY: December 6

Milan. No English equivalent. Slavic. "Nice, dear, beloved."
Today, this name is more popular among the Slovaks and
Serbo-Croatians than among the Poles.

DIMINUTIVE: None

FEAST DAYS: May 19, June 18

Mirosław. No English equivalent. Slavic. Two-part name
consisting of "peace" + "fame, glory, renown."
First appeared in Polish records in 1202, then as the
shortened forms *Mirek* (1210), *Mirosz* (1219–1220), and
Miroszek (1265). A name that continues to find favor today.

DIMINUTIVES: Mirek, Mireczek

FEAST DAY: February 26

Napoleon. Napoleon. Latin. "One from Naples."
The name honors Napoleon Bonaparte who figured largely
in Polish history as the commander of Polish troops in his

Grand Army during the Napoleonic Wars. In Poland, it is used as a first or middle name. Napoleon Ignacy Rafał Czerwiakowski (1802–1882) wrote the first handbook on botany in Poland.

DIMINUTIVE: None

FEAST DAY: August 15

Narcyz. Narcissus. Greek. "The narcissus flower." This name appeared in Polish records in 1495. It resurfaced in the 19TH and 20TH centuries, but was only somewhat popular.

DIMINUTIVE: None

FEAST DAYS: March 18, September 17, October 29

Nicefor. No English equivalent. Greek. Two-part name consisting of "victory" + "bring."
Came to Poland from the Latin *Nicephorus*. The Russian spelling is *Nikifor*.

DIMINUTIVE: None

FEAST DAYS: February 9, March 1

Niecisław. No English equivalent. Slavic. Two-part name consisting of "to kindle, arouse" + "fame, glory, renown."
A name which originated in the 19TH century.

DIMINUTIVE: None

FEAST DAY: July 15

Nikodem. Nicodemus. Greek. Two-part name consisting of "victory" + "people."

This name was common in Poland throughout the centuries as both a first and middle name. Nikodem Muśnicki (1765–1805) was a playwright and poet. Napoleon Nikodem Cybulski (1854–1919) was a professor at Jagiellonian University. Only recently has the name fallen out of favor.

DIMINUTIVES: Nik, Nikuś
FEAST DAYS: May 3, June 13

Norbert. Norbert. Old German. Two-part name consisting of "north" + "brilliant, shining."

DIMINUTIVES: Norbercik, Bercik, Bert
FEAST DAY: June 6

Oktawiusz. Octavius. Latin. "Eighth."
DIMINUTIVE: Oktawiuszek
FEAST DAY: November 20

Onufry. Humphrey. Old German. "Peace, peaceful Hun."
An old-fashioned name which enjoyed tremendous popularity at the end of the 18TH century.
DIMINUTIVE: Nufcio
FEAST DAY: June 12

Pabian. See **Fabian**.

Pakosław. No English equivalent. Slavic. Two-part name
consisting of "greater" + "fame, glory, renown."
Appeared in Polish documents as early as 1145 and as late
as the 17ᵀᴴ century.
DIMINUTIVE: None
FEAST DAY: February 15

Pankracy. Pancratius. Greek. Two-part name consisting of
"all" + "strong, mighty."
St. Pancras is the patron saint of children receiving their
first communion. Most Poles associate Pankracy with three
feast days which usher in spring: St. Pankracy (May 12),
St. Serwacy (May 13), and St. Bonifacy (May 14).
DIMINUTIVE: None
FEAST DAY: May 12

Paweł. Paul. Latin. "Little."
A common name in all Christian lands from the Middle
Ages until today. It was the name of seven different popes
as well as Russian emperors. St. Paul wrote fourteen books
of the New Testament and is honored with St. Peter as the
co-founder of the Holy Roman Catholic Church.
DIMINUTIVE: Pawlik
FEAST DAY: June 29

Pelagiusz. Pelagius. Greek. "Of the sea."

A rare name in Poland.

DIMINUTIVE: None

FEAST DAY: October 8

❖ ❖ ❖

Petroniusz. Petronius. Latin. "Member of the clan of Petronia."

In Poland, it is best known as the name of the Roman in Henryk Sienkiewicz's Nobel Prize-winning book *Quo Vadis*.

DIMINUTIVE: None

FEAST DAY: October 4

❖ ❖ ❖

Piotr. Peter. Greek. "Rock."

In the Bible, Simon was a fisherman in the Sea of Galilee. Jesus renamed Simon as Cephas, the Aramaic equivalent of the Greek word meaning "Peter" (rock) in English. Jesus said: "On this rock I will build my church . . . and I will give you the keys of the Kingdom." St. Peter was the first bishop of Rome.

DIMINUTIVES: Piotrek, Piotruś

FEAST DAY: June 29

❖ ❖ ❖

Polikarp. Polycarp. Greek. "Fruitful."

Came to Poland from the Latin *Policarpus*. Can be used as a first or middle name.

DIMINUTIVES: Polikarpek, Karp

FEAST DAY: January 26

❖ ❖ ❖

Przemysł. No English equivalent. Slavic. Two-part name
consisting of "through" + "mind, thought."
The name of several Polish princes.
DIMINUTIVE: Przemek
FEAST DAYS: April 13, September 4

Przemysław. No English equivalent. Slavic. Two-part name
consisting of "mind, thought" + "fame, glory, renown."
DIMINUTIVES: Przemek, Sławek
FEAST DAYS: April 13, September 4

Radosław. No English equivalent. Slavic. Two-part name
consisting of "glad" + "fame, glory, renown."
Various forms of this name appeared in the Middle Ages,
including *Redosław* (1324).
DIMINUTIVE: None
FEAST DAY: March 2

Rafał. Raphael, Rafael. Hebrew. "God heals."
St. Raphael is one of the three archangels mentioned in the
Bible. The name also appeared in Polish documents as
Rafael (1224), *Rachał* (1424), and *Refael* (1435).
DIMINUTIVE: Rafałek
FEAST DAY: September 29

Rajmund. Raymond, Raymund. Old German. "Protector."
A common name in Silesia.
DIMINUTIVES: Rajmundek, Mundek, Mundzik
FEAST DAYS: January 7 & 23

❖ ❖ ❖

Robert. Robert, Robin. Old German. Two-part name
consisting of "fame" + "brilliant, shining."
A name known to Poland since the Middle Ages, but only
achieved popularity within the last two centuries. More
popular among the Germans and the English.
DIMINUTIVES: Robcio, Robercik
FEAST DAYS: January 26, April 17 & 29, June 7

❖ ❖ ❖

Roch. No English equivalent. Old German. Meaning of the
name is unclear.
The patron saint of contagious diseases. An old-fashioned
Polish name. According to legend, Roch lived in the
14TH century and devoted his life to caring for the sick; he
cured many by making the sign of the cross over them.
DIMINUTIVE: None
FEAST DAY: August 17

❖ ❖ ❖

Roland. Roland, Rowland. Old German. Two-part name
consisting of "fame" + "land, country."
Some variations of the name have included *Ruland* (1360)
and *Rorand* (1402).
DIMINUTIVE: None
FEAST DAY: September 15

❖ ❖ ❖

Roman. Roman. Latin. "One from Rome."

Originally *Romanus*, the name belonged to a Roman who lived as a hermit and developed a following. Known in Poland since the 12TH century, as well as in Russia and the Byzantine Empire.

DIMINUTIVE: Romek

FEAST DAY: February 28

Ryszard. Richard. Old German. "Hard ruler."

Richard is a name that often evokes images of Richard the Lion-Hearted and Shakespearean plays. The name has adopted many forms in Poland over the centuries, including *Rykard* (1212), *Rychard* (1222), and *Rejchart* (1385).

DIMINUTIVES: Ryś, Rysiek, Rysio

FEAST DAYS: February 7, April 3, October 25

S

Sebastian. Sebastian. Greek. "Honorable, dignified."

St. Sebastian was a Roman soldier who suffered a martyr's death. He is considered the patron saint of the wounded and contagiously ill. A popular name among 18TH century nobility and people living in Podhale.

DIMINUTIVES: Bastek, Sobek, Sobuś

FEAST DAY: January 20

Serafin. Seraphinus. Hebrew. "Flaming ones."

St. Seraphinus was a member of the Order of Friars Minor Capuchin (orig. 1529), an austere branch of the first order of St. Francis of Assisi engaged in missionary work and preaching. He was canonized in 1767.

DIMINUTIVE: None

FEAST DAYS: July 29, October 12 & 29

Serwacy. Servais, Servatius. Latin. "Saved, rescued."

Known in Poland, but not widespread. A name associated with St. Pankracy (May 12) and St. Bonifacy (May 14) who, according to Polish folk tradition, usher in spring.

DIMINUTIVE: None

FEAST DAY: May 13

Seweryn. Severin. Latin. "One from Severus."

A well-liked name in Poland during the 19TH century.

DIMINUTIVE: None

FEAST DAYS: January 8, November 19

Siemowit. See **Ziemowit**.

Sławomir. No English equivalent. Slavic. Two-part name consisting of "fame, glory, renown" + "peace."

A popular name until the 16TH century, and then experienced a revival in the 19TH century.

DIMINUTIVES: Sław, Sławek
FEAST DAY: May 17

Sofroniusz. Sophron. Greek. "Sensible, sound mind."
A more popular name among eastern Slavs.
DIMINUTIVE: None
FEAST DAY: March 11

Stanisław. Stanislas, Stanislaus. Slavic. Two-part name
consisting of "become" + "fame, glory, renown."
A favorite Polish name for boys since ancient times, its
popularity has not diminished over the centuries. Spelling
variations have included *Stanek* (1242) and *Stacher* (1442).
Its popularity was aided by two Polish saints: Stanisław
Szczepanowski, bishop of Cracow (*c*. 1030–1079), and
St. Stanisław Kostka (1550–1568). The latter vowed to
become a Jesuit. When his family forbade the vocation,
he walked all the way to Rome. He received Holy Orders
when he was seventeen years old, but died within a year.
DIMINUTIVES: Staszek, Stach, Stasio
FEAST DAYS: April 11, August 14, November 13

Stefan. Stephen, Steven. Greek. "Crown."
St. Stephen was the first martyr of the Church. A popular
name both in Poland and in Hungary.
DIMINUTIVES: Stefanek, Stefek
FEAST DAY: December 26

Stojan. No English equivalent. Slavic. "Stand."
Appeared in Polish records in 1244, but was rarely used. A
more common name among Bulgarians, Slovaks, and
Serbo-Croatians.
DIMINUTIVE: None
FEAST DAY: May 7

Świętosław. No English equivalent. Slavic. Two-part name
consisting of "mighty" + "fame, glory, renown."
A very popular name during the Middle Ages and
remaining so until the 18TH century.
DIMINUTIVE: None
FEAST DAY: August 31

Sylwester. Sylvester, Silvester. Latin. "From the wooded area."
New Year's Eve in Poland is called "Sylvester" after a saint
who was Bishop of Rome in 314. St. Sylvester recognized
Christianity and ended persecution against it. The name of
three different popes.
DIMINUTIVES: Sylwek, Sylwuś
FEAST DAY: December 31

Szczepan. See **Stefan**.

Szymon. Simon, Simeon. Hebrew. "Listening."
St. Simon was one of the twelve apostles. A very common
and well-liked name in Poland from the Middle Ages until

the 18TH century. Currently enjoying a resurgence in
popularity.
DIMINUTIVE: Szymek
FEAST DAY: October 28

Tadeusz. Thaddeus. Hebrew. "Courageous, valiant."
In old Polish records this name appeared in the shortened
forms *Tadej* (1339) and *Tadaj* (1430). A more popular name
in Lithuania. St. Thaddeus was one of the lesser known of
the twelve apostles.
DIMINUTIVES: Tadek, Tadzio
FEAST DAY: October 28

Teobald. Theobald, Tibald. Old German. Two-part name
consisting of "clan, tribe" + "bold, brave."
A name encountered in 13TH and 15TH century Polish
documents. St. Teobald is the patron saint of charcoal burners.
According to legend he, himself, worked at such tasks.
DIMINUTIVE: None
FEAST DAY: June 30

Teodor. Theodore. Greek. "God's gift."
St. Theodore was put to death for refusing to denounce his
faith. A well-liked name in Poland for many centuries.

DIMINUTIVE: Dorek
FEAST DAY: February 7

◈ ◈ ◈

Teofil. Theophil. Greek. "Dear to God."
More common in 19TH and 20TH century Poland than today.
In Silesia, *Teoś* is used as a nickname.
DIMINUTIVES: Teofilik, Fil, Filek
FEAST DAYS: January 20, April 27, October 2

◈ ◈ ◈

Tobiasz. Tobias. Hebrew. "The Lord is good."
Common in Poland from the 13TH through the 18TH centuries,
but less so today.
DIMINUTIVE: None
FEAST DAY: September 9

◈ ◈ ◈

Tomasz. Thomas. Aramaic. "Twin."
Doubting Thomas, one of the apostles, refused to recognize
the risen Christ unless he could see and feel the marks of
the Crucifixion. The name of some of the most famous
religious men throughout the centuries: St. Thomas Becket,
archbishop of Canterbury, St. Thomas Acquinas, and
St. Thomas More.
DIMINUTIVES: Tomek, Tomko
FEAST DAYS: January 28, June 22, July 3, December 29

◈ ◈ ◈

Tomisław. No English equivalent. Slavic. Two-part name
consisting of "to torment" + "fame, glory, renown."

Appeared in Polish records in 1198. Experienced a revival in the 19TH century, when old Slavic names regained popularity.
DIMINUTIVE: None
FEAST DAY: December 21

Tymon. Timon. Greek. "Honor."
Appeared infrequently as the shortened forms *Temo* (1242) and *Tymo* (1253) in old Polish documents.
DIMINUTIVE: None
FEAST DAY: September 28

Tytus. Titus. Latin. "Wild pigeon."
A name encountered among the first families of Poland in the 18TH and 19TH centuries, i.e. Tytus Działyński. Tytus Chałbiński was a physician and naturalist who made Zakopane a famous health resort.
DIMINUTIVE: None
FEAST DAYS: January 4 & 6, February 2

U

Urban. Urban. Latin. "Citizen."
St. Urban is the patron saint of vintners. The name of eight popes.
DIMINUTIVES: Urbanek, Urbaś
FEAST DAYS: May 19 & 25

Wacław. Wenceslaus. Slavic. Two-part name consisting of "more" + "fame, glory, renown."
Grandson of St. Ludmiła, Wenceslaus worked for the conversion of pagans in Czechoslovakia. A popular name throughout the centuries in Poland, but more so in Slovakia where he is considered their patron saint.
DIMINUTIVES: Wacek, Wacławek
FEAST DAY: September 28

Waldemar. Valdemar. German. Two-part name consisting of "to rule" + "famous."
Shortened versions of this name, *Waldek* and *Waldko*, surfaced in the 14TH century. The full name appeared in the 19TH century.
DIMINUTIVES: Waldek, Waldeczek, Waldzio
FEAST DAY: May 5

Walenty, **Walentyn**. Valentine. Latin. "Mighty, valiant."
St. Valentine is the patron saint of engaged couples. A prominent name for Polish men at one time, it has since fallen out of favor.
DIMINUTIVE: Walek
FEAST DAY: February 14

Walerian. Valerian. Latin. "Belonging to Valerius."
A common name throughout the centuries, but less so in
recent years.
DIMINUTIVE: Walerek
FEAST DAYS: January 29, April 14

❖ ❖ ❖

Walter. Walter. Old German. Two-part name consisting of
"rule" + "lord."
Also spelled *Waltheras* (1149–1150) and *Waltyr* (1456).
DIMINUTIVE: None
FEAST DAYS: May 2, June 5

❖ ❖ ❖

Wawrzyniec. Laurence, Lawrence. Latin. "Of Laurentum."
St. Lawrence was a deacon who was martyred and
developed a following in Europe. A favorite boys' name
among the Polish nobility.
DIMINUTIVE: Wawrzek
FEAST DAY: August 10

❖ ❖ ❖

Wiesław. No English equivalent. Slavic. Meaning unclear,
but thought to come from an old Russian two-part name
consisting of "all" + "fame, glory, renown."
Often, Poles took the name *Wesley* in English-speaking
countries.
DIMINUTIVES: Wiesiek, Wiesio
FEAST DAYS: May 22, June 7, December 9

❖ ❖ ❖

Wiktor. Victor. Latin. "Conqueror, victory."
Name taken by four popes and one saint.
DIMINUTIVES: Wicio, Witek, Wituś
FEAST DAYS: March 6, April 12, July 28, September 16

Wilhelm. William. Old German. "Strong fighter."
Appeared in this particular form in Poland as early as 1153,
and then as *Wilhalm* (1365) and *Wilham* (1479). Continued
to be popular in Silesia where German influence was
significant.
DIMINUTIVES: Wilek, Wiluś
FEAST DAYS: April 6, June 25

Wincenty. Vincent. Latin. "Conquering."
A name made famous by St. Vincent de Paul, a Frenchman
who founded the Vincentian Congregation, a society of
priests devoted to missionary work. It was also the name
of one of Poland's most famous chroniclers, Wincenty
Kadłubek, who was also bishop of Cracow (1150?–1223).
He was beatified in 1764.
DIMINUTIVE: Wicek
FEAST DAY: September 27

Wisław. No English equivalent. Slavic. Two-part name
consisting of "lord" + "fame, glory, renown."
DIMINUTIVE: None
FEAST DAY: June 6

Wit. No English equivalent. Origin unclear, but thought to be connected to the Latin *vitus*. "Willing."
The name appeared as early as 1228 in this particular form, and as *Wito* in 1483. Since the Middle Ages, St. Wit was known as the patron saint of apothecaries, artists, miners, and those who suffered from a shaking disorder that came to be called "St. Witus Dance." Wit Stwosz (*c.* 1447–1533) was the sculptor of the famous triptych on the high altar of St. Mary's Church in Cracow.
DIMINUTIVE: None
FEAST DAY: June 15

Witold. Witold. Lithuanian. Two-part name consisting of "shepherd" + "people."
This name is quite popular today.
DIMINUTIVES: Witek, Tolek, Tolo
FEAST DAYS: June 15, November 12

Władysław. No English equivalent. Slavic. Two-part name consisting of "to rule" + "fame, glory, renown."
Perhaps the meaning of this name is the reason why it was favored by kings of Poland and by ruling classes of Bohemia and Hungary. Extremely popular boys' name in Poland unlike its female counterpart.
DIMINUTIVES: Włada, Władeczek, Władek, Władzio
FEAST DAYS: June 27, September 25

Włodzimierz. Vladimir. Slavic. Two-part name consisting of "to rule" + "peace."

Popular among eastern Slavs due to Vladimir the Great, Prince of Kiev in the 10TH century.

DIMINUTIVES: Włodek, Włodeczek, Włodzio

FEAST DAY: January 16

Wojciech. Adalbert, Adelbert, Albert. Slavic. Two-part name consisting of "warrior" + "joy."

Appeared in Polish documents as *Wociech* (1275), *Wojch* (1293), *Wojciek* (1399), and *Wojtasz* (1428). One of Poland's most popular boys' names due to St. Adalbert, martyr and patron saint of Pomerania and Great Poland.

DIMINUTIVES: Wojtek, Wojtul, Wojteczek

FEAST DAY: April 23

Wojsław. No English equivalent. Slavic. Two-part name consisting of "warrior" + "courageous."

This name had various spellings over the centuries, including *Wojisław* (12TH century) and *Wojesław* (1425).

DIMINUTIVE: None

FEAST DAYS: January 26, March 5, October 8

Zachariasz. Zachariah, Zechariah, Zacharias, Zachary.
Hebrew. "Remembered by God."
St. Zachary was the father of St. John the Baptist. A popular
name among Orthodox Slavs.
DIMINUTIVE: None
FEAST DAY: November 5

Zbigniew. No English equivalent. Slavic. Two-part
name consisting of "to get rid of, dispense with" +
"anger, wrath."
An ancient name that resurfaced in the 19ᵀᴴ century when
old Slavic names regained popularity. One of the heroes in
Henryk Sienkiewicz's novel *Teutonic Knights* is called by
the diminutive *Zbyszko*.
DIMINUTIVES: Zbyszek, Zbyszko, Zbysio
FEAST DAY: March 17

Zdzisław. No English equivalent. Slavic. Two-part
name consisting of "to lay down, set down" + "fame,
glory, renown."
First appeared in this form in the 12ᵀᴴ century, and then
more commonly in its diminutive forms: *Zdzisz* (1386),
Zdziszio (1386), *Zdziesz* (1398), and *Zdzisiek* (1404).
Formerly one of Poland's most popular boys' names, it is
now decreasing in use.

DIMINUTIVES: Zdzich, Zdziś, Zdzisio, Zdisiek, Zdzisek
FEAST DAYS: January 29, November 29

Zenobiusz. Zenobius. Greek. Two-part name consisting of "Zeus" + "life."
An uncommon name in Poland.
DIMINUTIVES: Zenek, Zenio, Zenus
FEAST DAYS: February 20, December 4

Zenon. Zeno. Greek. "Gift of Zeus."
Well-liked in the early 1900s, but now considered an old-fashioned name.
DIMINUTIVES: Zenek, Zenio, Zenuś
FEAST DAYS: February 14, June 23, December 22

Ziemowit. No English equivalent. Slavic. Two-part name consisting of "person, family" + "lord, master."
Ziemowit was the legendary great-grandson of Mieszko I, the first king of Poland. This name appeared in Polish documents dating from the 12ᵀᴴ century. The original name was **Siemowit**, but over time it changed, becoming the form that exists today.
DIMINUTIVE: None
FEAST DAY: October 18

Zygfryd. Siegfried. Old German. Two-part name consisting of "victory" + "peace."

St. Sigfrid is the patron saint of Sweden, where he helped to renew Christianity. This Polish version of a German name was spelled in a variety of ways, including *Sifrit* (1228), *Cyfryt* (1260), and *Zajfryt* (1477). A more common name in Silesia.

DIMINUTIVES: Frydek, Frydzio

FEAST DAY: February 15

Zygmunt. Sigmund. Old German. Two-part name consisting of "victory" + "protection."

An old Polish name that often was handed down through the centuries to princes in line for the Polish throne. It appears to have come to Poland through the Czechs. Various spellings have included *Zygmont* (1433) and *Sigismund* (1438).

DIMINUTIVES: Zyga, Zyguś

FEAST DAY: May 2

Other Polish Titles from Hippocrene . . .

Polish Fables: Bilingual Edition
Ignacy Krasicki, Translated by Gerard T. Kapolka

Ignacy Krasicki (1735-1801) was hailed as "The Prince of Poets" by his contemporaries. With great artistry the author used contemporary events and human relations to show a course to guide human conduct. For over two centuries, Krasicki's fables have entertained and instructed his delighted readers. This bilingual gift edition contains the original Polish text with side-by-side English translation. Twenty illustrations by Barbara Swidzinska, a well known Polish artist, add to the volume's charm.

105 pages • 6 x 9 • 20 illustrations • 0-7818-0548-1 • W • $19.95hc • (646)

Treasury of Polish Aphorisms: Bilingual Edition
Compiled and Translated by Jacek Galazka, Introduction by Jerzy R. Krzyzanowski

This collection comprises 225 aphorisms by eighty Polish writers, many of them well known in their native land. Sixteen pen and ink drawings by talented Polish illustrator Barbara Swidzinska complete this remarkable exploration of true Polish wit and wisdom.

140 pages • 5 x 8 • 20 illustrations • 0-7818-0549-X • W • $14.95hc • (647)

Dictionary of 1,000 Polish Proverbs: Bilingual Edition
Edited by Miroslaw Lipinski

In this volume, the proverbs are arranged side-by-side with their English translations. The collection is organized alphabetically by key word, with an index listing the proverbs by English subject.
131 pages • 5 x 8 • 0-7818-0482-5 • W • $11.95pb • (568)

Treasury of Polish Love Poems, Quotations and Proverbs: Bilingual Edition
Editor and Translator Miroslaw Lipinski

This collection includes endearing quotes and enlightening wisdom from Poland's greatest poets, writers and aphorists: Adam Mickiewicz, Zygmunt Krasinski, Julian Tuwim, Boleslaw Prus and Henryk Sienkiewicz, to name a few. See companion cassettes.
128 pages • 0-7818-0297-0 • $11.95 • (185)

Treasury of Polish Love Poems, Quotations and Proverbs: Bilingual Edition
Audio Book (Cassettes)

The romantic musings of more than 40 Polish writers are included in this audio book in Polish and English, providing students with an immediate translation of each work. The selections are read in Polish by Marta Jurasz and Krzysztof Stawowy, members of the Cracow Artistic Ensemble and in English by Ken Kliban, an experienced actor with Broadway and voice credits.
2 Cassettes • 0-7818-0361-6 • $12.95 • (576)

**Treasury of Love Poems by Adam Mickiewicz
In Polish and English**
Edited by Krystyna Olszer

This beautiful bilingual gift edition contains 31 poems and longer excerpts, with 14 new translations by Stanislaw Baranczak, Clare Cavanaugh and Michael J. Mikos.

137 pages • Polish and English text side-by-side • 0-7818-0652-6 • $11.95hc • (735)

Polish Customs, Traditions & Folklore: Revised Edition
Sophie H. Knab, Introduction by Rev. Czeslaw Krysa

This unique reference is arranged by month, showing the various occasions, feasts and holidays prominent in Polish culture—beginning with December it continues through Holy Week Customs, superstitions, beliefs and rituals associated with farming, Pentecost, Corpus Christi, midsummer, harvest festival, wedding rites, namedays, birth and death. Line illustrations complete this rich and varied treasury of folklore. Now updated with new chapter on "Custom for Kids"!

340 pages • 0-7818-0515-5 • $22.50hc • (500)

Polish Wedding Customs and Traditions
Sophie Hodorowicz Knab

From bestselling author, Sophie Hodorowicz Knab, comes this unique planning guide for Americans who want to organize and celebrate a Polish-style wedding. Sections titled Engagement, Bridal Flowers, Wedding Clothes, Ceremony, Reception and even Baby Names, will assist the bride and groom-to-be through every step of the wedding process. Special tips on

"How to Draw from the Past" at the end of each chapter provide helpful suggestions on how to incorporate Polish tradition into the modern wedding, to make it a truly distinctive and unforgettable event. Photographs and illustrations are also included throughout the book.

196 pages • 6 x 9 • photos/illustrations • 0-7818-0530-9 • W • $19.95hc • (641)

Hippocrene Children's Illustrated Polish Dictionary

As Polish is one of the less commonly taught languages in the U.S., it is sometimes difficult for the parents to pass their native language to their children. This dictionary is the first step to teach children of the Polish descent the language of their ancestors.

94 pages • 8 x 11 • 500 entries • illustrations in color • 0-7818-0711-5 • W • $14.95hc • (799)

The Best of Polish Cooking: Revised Edition
A Hippocrene Original Cookbook
Karen West

"A charming offering of Polish cuisine with lovely woodcuts throughout the book."—*Publisher's Weekly*

219 pages • 5 x 8 • 0-87052-932-3 • W • $8.95pb • (391)

Old Polish Traditions in the Kitchen and at the Table
Lemnis & Vitry

A cookbook and a history of Polish culinary customs. Short essays cover subjects like Polish hospitality, holiday traditions even the exalted status of the mushroom. Included are over 100 recipes for traditional family fare.

304 pages • 5 x 8 • 0-7818-0488-4 • W • $11.95pb • (546)

Polish Heritage Cookery: Illustrated Edition
A Hippocrene Original Cookbook
Robert & Maria Strybel

New illustrated edition of the bestseller with 20 color photographs! Over 2,200 recipes in 29 categories, written especially for Americans!

"Polish Heritage Cookery is the best [Polish] cookbook printed on the English market! It's well organized, informative, interlaced with historical background on Polish foods and eating habits, with easy-to-follow recipes readily prepared in American kitchens and, above all, it's fun to read."

—*Polish American Cultural Network*

915 pages • 16 pages of color photographs • 0-7818-0558-9 • $39.95hc • (658)

Polish Cuisine (Bilingual)
A Hippocrene Original Cookbook
Maria de Gorgey

Polish cuisine is noted for its hearty and satisfying offerings, and this charming bilingual cookbook brings the best of traditional Polish cooking to your table—with recipes in Polish and English! Among the chapters included are Soups and Appetizers, Main Courses, Desserts, and two special holiday chapters—one voted to "Wigilia," the festive Polish Christmas Eve Dinner, and

one devoted to "Wielkanoc," the Polish Easter Luncheon. All 60 recipes are adapted for the modern North American kitchen.
146 pages • 5 x 7 • 0-7818-0738-7 • $11.95hc • W • (151)

Polish Heritage Songbook
Compiled by Marek Sart, Illustrated by Szymon Kobylinski, Annotated by Stanislaw Werner

This unique collection of 74 songs is a treasury of nostalgia, capturing echoes of a long struggle for freedom carried out by generations of Polish men and women. The annotations are in English, the songs are in Polish.
166 pages • 6 x 9 • 65 illustrations • 74 songs • 0-7818-0425-6 • $14.95pb • (496)

Polish Folk Dances & Songs: A Step by Step Guide
Ada Dziewanowska

The most comprehensive and definitive book on Polish dance in the English language, with in-depth descriptions of over 80 of Poland's most characteristic and interesting dances. The author provides step-by-step instructions on positions, basic steps, and patterns for each dance. Includes over 400 illustrations depicting steps and movements and over 90 appropriate musical selections.
670 pages • 400 illustrations • 0-7818-0420-5 • $39.50hc • (580)

Song, Dance, and Customs of Peasant Poland
Sula Benet, Preface by Margaret Mead

Concentrating on the regions of present day Poland, the author presents the basic portrait of peasants and peasant ways throughout the diverse, elastic and curiously consistent area that is Poland.

247 pages • 6 x 9 • illustrations • 0-7818-0447-7
• $24.95hc • (209)

Polish Folk Embroidery
Jadwiga Turska

190 stunning full-color illustrations showcase the folk art of Poland's 31 regions, from Krakow to Podhale, from Silesia to Lowicz, from Mazovia, Kashubia, to Kuyavia and Kurpie; a striking display of folk costumes, furnishings, headgear and decorations. A glossary of terms and a bibliography are included.

360 pages • 8 x 3 • 190 color illustrations • 0-7818-0719-0
• $75.00hc • NA • (780)

All prices subject to change without prior notice. To purchase Hippocrene Books contact your local bookstore, call (718) 454-2366, or write to: **HIPPOCRENE BOOKS**, 171 Madison Avenue, New York, NY 10016. Please enclose check or money order, adding $5.00 shipping (UPS) for the first book and $.50 for each additional book.